"Finding the Goalposts": Masculinities through Sports Clubs in Upington

Samuel Julius

Langaa Research & Publishing CIG
Mankon, Bamenda

Publisher:
Langaa RPCIG
Langaa Research & Publishing Common Initiative Group
P.O. Box 902 Mankon
Bamenda
North West Region
Cameroon
Langaagrp@gmail.com
www.langaa-rpcig.net

Distributed in and outside N. America by
African Books Collective
orders@africanbookscollective.com
www.africanbookscollective.com

ISBN-10: 9956-554-44-8

ISBN-13: 978-9956-554-44-7

Acknowledgements

For months I have been eagerly anticipating this part of the writing project. This book is an amalgamation of the effort, sacrifices and love of so many people in the communities which make me. I am forever indebted to you. My gratitude overflows.

To my parents, Sammy and Sophia Julius, who lovingly raised me and taught me what is truly important in life. My mother was my first (and undoubtedly best) teacher. She is a genius. She helped instil in me a love for knowledge, writing and the arts. My father continues to show me what it means to be a selfless and gentle man, my role model for the father I wish to be one day. I love you both so much. Thank you for loving me.

To my siblings, Sean and Samantha, for teaching, supporting, pushing, motivating, humbling and even just accommodating me since childhood. I appreciate you more than I care to admit. Thank you for guiding me. I will always have the time of day for both of you.

To Esmeralda, my better half, for teaching me what it means to be resilient and approaching life with optimism even in the face of adversity. Thank you for allowing me to learn from, and annoy you every day. You push me to be a better person. Thank you for believing in me. I cannot wait to see you soon. I love you.

To Ariella, Esther, Chase, Kwoba, Kitty – and Señora Esther and Señor Rosalino in their temporary absence – thank you for allowing me to stay in your home and share yourself and your space so graciously with me. I wrote the first chapter of this book in Brooklyn, while waiting for Esme to return from work. Your warmth made it a comforting experience, and gave me a sense of home away from home. May God bless your family and respective journeys for years to come.

To Kathy and Gideon, the Mellon Mays Undergraduate Fellowship coordinators, thank you for seeing my potential and taking a gamble on me. Your support and guidance are invaluable. You are the academic aunty and uncle that I can rely on. You have given me a trove of memories that shaped my life forever. A special thank you for allowing me to get on a plane for the first time!

To my MMUF family, Faaria, Jordan, Lilitha and Haytham. You are some of the most magical people I've ever met. Your friendship helped carry me through the past years of university and beyond. I cannot imagine my life without your humour and kindness. You were the ones I had been waiting for. Thank you for being a part of something special.

To Isabella, for reading through my ideas and diligently honing them with your skill and intelligence. I am so grateful for your patience and warmth. Thank you for wanting the best for all of us, and being a truly caring person. Having worked with you, I see first-hand the excellence and simultaneous humility you exude.

To Ayanda, my mentor, for your open-door policy and your patience and genuine love. This project took shape in our meetings and wouldn't have been possible without you. Thank you for imparting your wisdom, being so willing to listen to my naïve ramblings, and treating me as though I mattered. I look up to you.

To Francis, who supervised this project. Thank you for enabling my dreams, believing in me and this work and enriching our beautiful continent with your thoughts, perseverance and selfless passion. Your humility and cheerful nature is refreshing. I remember being nervous to meet with you because of your incredible work and status as a true academic grootman. Thank you for encouraging my ideas and sharing your academic prowess with me. Your interest, feedback, support and implicit life lessons made this project a joy to produce.

To Uncle John and Aunty Rose, who graciously hosted me for most of my stay in Upington. Your hospitality and care are reflected in every corner of your home. Thank you for making this project possible. I could never repay you. Thank you for incorporating me into your family. My gratitude cannot be exemplified in words. To Yohniveve, for the walks to school or to the mall, and for treating me like a brother and taking care of me. I love you, cousin. You are the strongest person I know. It is an honour to be in your presence.

To Sithe and the Upington City team, thank you for allowing me to talk to you and get to know you. I wish you the best of luck as you navigate the heights of South African football.

To Coach Ash and the DFC team, thank you for accommodating me, letting me in and making me feel at home with your club. Your kindness radiates throughout the club. Every one of you treated me with the utmost respect. Thank you all for sharing your perspectives and opinions. You have gained a fan for life.

To my wider family in Upington, the Strauss family, Steenkamp family and Ouma Anna in particular, thank you for sharing your time with me and treating me with love. I love you all and hope to see you soon.

To the rest of my family and friends in Cape Town, the Julius Family, the Masters family, the Steenberg Seventh-Day Adventist Church, Nathanael, Jayden and Bryce, and everyone else who plays an indelible role in my life and subsequently in this project, thank you for your friendship and guidance. I am because you are.

To Langaa Publishers, thank you for publishing this ethnography and sowing seeds of knowledge into the future. May your efforts never be in vain, and your labour rewarded for generations to come. Thank you for dreaming so boldly and not settling for anything but the highest standards in the pursuit of a more just future.

To Dr. Morrell, for being willing to meet with me and collaborate on the preface. I remember how scared I was of saying something stupid when we met, owing to the impact of your work. Thank you for being kind, asking me questions and reading my work. Your review means more to me than you realise.

To my classmates and the entire faculty of Anthropology at the University of Cape Town. Thank you for making campus such a pleasant place. Our discussions are so engaging and you all have such important contributions to make in the world. If you ever find yourself in Upington during the holidays, my number has been attached above.

Finally, to the One without whom nothing is possible, God. May all glory and honour go to you. Thank you for giving me the strength to undertake this project. My entire existence is owed to you. Thank you for being the source of all good things. Thank you for the people you have placed in my path. Your mercy to me knows no bounds. May this project, and my life, be a meaningful blessing to all who encounter it. Amen.

Table of Contents

Preface

Robert Morrell

South Africa is a country with a population passionate about sport. Perhaps the country has hit its zenith with a rugby team crowned world rugby champions twice in a row (2019 and 2023) led by an iconic captain, Siya Kolisi. The popularity of the sport can be assessed by two books about Kolisi and one about the coach, Rassie Erasmus, appearing within five years (2019-2024); to sold out crowds and the two series Supersport TV series, Chasing the Sun. But possibly the clinching moment was Kolisi's statement accepting the 2023 World Cup that he 'did it for the people of South Africa'.

Below and hardly visible beneath the heights of international rugby, lie levels of competitive rugby (and soccer) drawing tens of thousands of South African players into these two games. Samuel Julius in this book offers deep insights into these levels of the game, bringing them to life as he mingles with soccer and rugby players of the dusty, hot town of Upington in the Northern Cape.

Samuel is a Cape Town boy but with a good chunk of his heart residing in Upington where many of his family still live. In this book he takes his anthropological training together with a bag full of concepts from the field of Critical Men and Masculinities Studies (CMMS) and ensconces himself with two local sports teams, Defence Force Collegiates (rugby) and Upington City Football Club (soccer).

I love reading good anthropological research. And I particularly loved reading this book because Samuel has managed to enter the dimly lit corridors of masculinity and to shine his revealing light on the thoughts and feelings of the rugby and soccer players. This is terrain that has attracted much research and a lot of that gender research has sought to portray sport as the place of violence, oppression and exclusion. It is true that in South Africa sport has attracted research attention because of its nation-building achievements – both under apartheid (Grundlingh, Odendaal and Spies 1995) and more recently (Dickow and Moller 1999) – and hope of a non-racial future has been fuelled by players crossing racial boundaries (Bolsman and Parker 2007; Carton and Nauright 2015). But in terms of gender research much of the attention has remained on issues of violence and oppression. Of course, as Samuel himself readily concedes, this is important because the country is still, thirty years 'after apartheid', beset by world-leading levels of violence. And yet this approach has also fed into discourses of 'toxic masculinity' which easily feed into discourses about men being one-dimensional (and prone to aggression and violence).

Samuel, in this book, explores more salubrious angles and the book is certainly heart-warming as a result. To get below the surface of received wisdom about sport and about the locker room, Samuel asks questions that expose vulnerability and reveal tenderness, loyalty and much else. He shows how men seek to be 'useful men' and are determined to avoid becoming 'useless men'. How does one do this when one is black and in most case come from resource-poor environments with long histories of racial marginalization?

This book shows how bonds between team members are forged and maintained. How the team is more important than the individual. How reliability is central to success, how it is important to be accountable, to embrace one's role in the team and to mould and condition the body so that it can be of use to the team. These become the benchmarks of manhood.

These observations may sound obvious, but to scholars of masculinity they are not and they are contested. Samuel has done a wonderful job of framing his ethnography in debates about masculinities. He shows a confident grasp of these debates and how they have directed research in one direction rather than another and how this has resulted in blind spots that have prevented us from seeing the depth and importance of team sport participation at the local level.

Playing rugby and soccer is about success and achievement but it is also about so much more. The journey is often more important than the destination. How one becomes a team-member (and avoids being useless) is not a simple thing. It requires observing, accepting and enacting rituals. The handshake is very important – a sign of respect, of intimacy and of connection – and the handshake is exchanged many times amongst the players. There is not so much hugging which is to say that these young men also believe in boundaries and conservative gender etiquette. One sees this most clearly as Samuel tries to explore feelings about loss and care. A player dies from a rugby injury, a player's sister dies. What happens? There is a silence and a withdrawing, but there is also deep, often unstated sympathy and a willingness to admit to feelings of devastation.

Samuel is interested to understand what he calls activation of affect, following Hanspeter Reihling's important psychological exploration of men in the Western Cape (Reihling 2020). He explores the potential to do things differently and raises difficult topics to see if there is a vocabulary of emotion that allows men to escape prescriptions of what a man should and should not do. But Samuel's book is not about defying social norms, rather it is about how sportsmen find spaces to bond with other men, to support their friends, to care for themselves and for others.

The work of Francis Nyamnjoh, anthropologist and mentor, is central to this book. Francis has been developing the concept of 'incompleteness' for decades and in Samuel he has found a brilliant disciple who can use the concept to unlock the secrets of team sport. Incompleteness suggests that things are never concluded and that we are in a constant negotiation with ourselves and the world around us, with other people and with our own dreams. Incompleteness as concept allows Samuel to break through the rigidity of some approaches to masculinity research. Raewyn Connell's highly influential framework of hegemonic, complicit, subordinate and protest masculinities has always had the danger of becoming static, of fixing analysis at a moment in time as though that moment speaks for all time. Samuel's wonderful book shows that we are constantly working to be ourselves, to sustain organisations like sports teams, to juggle a host of often contradictory demands on our resources and emotions. And in the case of the Upington soccer and rugby teams, the results are that men get along with one another and find ways to be, and to see themselves as useful. Samuel calls this a process of becoming the 'new' South African man. This is a book that affirms rather than denigrates masculinity and gives us reason to believe that men can contribute to a safer, more fulfilling and more accepting world.

My final comment about this book is about its contribution to gender research in Africa. Samuel's work is pioneering a new approach to gender research in South Africa. He is steering a new and positive course by drawing on Nyamnjoh's work, on existing CMMS studies and by centring the importance of relationships in context. In this way he is also contributing to Southern Theory (Connell 2007). This theory suggests that research in the global South can contribute new insights and offer new perspectives that enrich understandings of social reality. By inviting us to Upington to experience the world through the eyes of its rugby and soccer players we are able to see how lives are lived, are created and how positive versions of being a man are enacted.

References

Bolsmann, C. and Parker, A. (2007) Soccer, South Africa and celebrity status: Mark Fish, popular culture and the post-apartheid state. *Soccer & Society*, 8(1): 109-124.

Carton, B. and J. Naurigh (2015) 'Last Zulu Warrior Standing': Cultural Legacies of Racial Stereotyping and Embodied Ethno-Branding in South Africa, *The International Journal of the History of Sport*, 32:7, 876-898.

Connell, R. (2007) *Southern Theory. The global dynamics of knowledge in social science* (Cambridge: Polity).

Dickow, H. and Møller, V. (2002) South Africa's Rainbow People', national pride and optimism: a trend study. *Social Indicators Research*, 59: 175-202.

Grundlingh, A. Odendaal, A. and B. Spies (1995) *Beyond the Tryline: Rugby and South African Society* (Johannesburg: Ravan).

Reihling, H. (2020) *Affective Health and Masculinities in South Africa. An Ethnography of (In)vulnerability* (London: Routledge).

Introduction

Sports clubs are an important structure in constructing sporting masculinities in Upington, a town at the heart of South Africa's Northern Cape. They serve as a frontier where masculinities shaped by different intersections of identity, negotiate and contest what is permissible for young men in the space. This book will argue that sports clubs shape and are shaped by interactions between club members. These interactions often revolve around a central theme of adhering to specialised responsibilities in order to negotiate masculine status. In addition, recognition rituals and responses to tragedy reveal the nuance of expression and community-building while delimiting appropriate forms of public touch and care. Masculinities are examined in tandem with interconnectivities and obligations to networks as partial, but important fulfilment of gendered subjectivities. This book draws on incompleteness as a useful conceptual framework. It is an incomplete work that merely aims to share stories and perspectives from within the sports club. It is a subjective attempt at grappling with racialised youth masculinities, and my own masculinities as a person embedded in these categories of identity. It aims to show the complexities and simplicities of masculinities that are often left out of popular narratives about young Black men in South Africa. This ethnography will begin by situating myself in the field and discussing the methodologies that inform this work.

Chapter 1

"Fieldtrips: Personal Prerogatives and Professional Prefacing in Upington"

Introduction

Historically, ethnographies have tended to focus on the writings of the Anthropologist during encounters in the field (Geertz, 1973). Paying attention to positionality and the illusion of impartiality in the field, this book begins with anecdotes and thoughts around how this research came about, and the factors that drove me to the field in the first place. This book is a collection of stories gathered around two sports clubs in the town of Upington, South Africa. It responds to the question: How do sports clubs influence conceptions and performances of masculinities amongst young men in Upington? This opening chapter begins by describing the allure of sports as an important intersection with South African masculinities, before delving into pain and its part in motivating this project. It introduces Upington to the reader in the ways in which I imagine the town and its portrayals in popular media. It then attempts to grapple with the subjectivities and truth claims implicit in ethnographic work. Finally, it delves into my own experiences with identity formation and masculinities in Upington and argues for the justification of this project as a necessary, incomplete work that reveals the complexities of the lived realities of sporting men in Upington, and the social structures influencing their performances. This opening chapter is decidedly personal and prefaces the chapter on methodologies with ethnographic sketches from before the research period.

Sport is a passion of mine. In the beginning of this research period, I looked towards my passions. I needed something to sustain me through the often-demoralising dread that accompanies deadlines and writer's block. I needed to study a phenomenon that was important to many, but also to me, and perhaps make a little more sense of the ever-emerging world and its confusions and contradictions. Like many other boys I knew in South Africa, I wanted to become a professional sportsperson[1]. The dream was there since before I could remember, reinforced by images of focused and then jubilant athletes, physical specimens with muscles on their muscles, "real, manly men". By the end of the first decade of life, many schoolboys in South Africa are driven by the ideal of physical prowess and sports as a marker for success as a man, particularly a heterosexual one (Bhana and Mayeza, 2016). This is historically contingent, and not merely a biological impulse (see Chapter 3). For me and, I suspect, a good deal of other boys, these ideals provided a source of solace in the event of pain through its various iterations.

Pain is hard to articulate and motivates different political and creative projects. Its wide-ranging forms are all played out in the body in some way (Scarry, 1985). Elaine Scarry (1985) highlights how pain's

---

[1] I was particularly enamoured by Cricket and spent many afternoons playing it with my siblings and school friends and reading autobiographies of players of yesteryear such as Allan Donald, Steve Waugh and Dermot Reeve, whom I appreciated through VHS tapes my Aunt had recorded from as early as 1996. I wanted to play cricket professionally. Mind you, I would have settled for being a footballer, tennis star, and later Formula 1 driver.

difficulty to be articulated[2] means it often receives less attention and visibility in more rigid public discourse, encouraging its expression in works of art and creation. Pain has also been a frighteningly effective motivator in my own life. My mother's painful hidings motivated me to stop certain delinquent actions and their consequences in future. The painful monologue one of my cousins received upon his failure to advance to his matric year of high school, fuelled a desire to take school more seriously to avoid more painful monologues directed at me. The pain of being perceived as a bad person, or worse, a useless one, motivated many of my people-pleasing habits that I am still in constant negotiation with. Pain, and figuring out how to navigate that pain in a way that does not reproduce the phenomenon, has a powerful influence on projects of sense-making and the construction of meaning in the world. Systems of meaning and value help offset, explain and reduce the pain that no-one can escape as a mortal and vulnerable being in this world (Peterson, 2018). While I am not attempting to make an existential argument, I do want to explain how this work came to be in an attempt to be forthright and expose the personal stakes which ultimately influence the direction of this research and my belief in its utility in the world.

Open Doors: Academic Conversations and Personal Revelations

This projects formal beginnings took place on a walk with Ayanda Manqoyi, a sterling Anthropologist

[2] It not only resists, but actively destroys language in its most painful moments when the person embodying that pain groans in agony (Scarry, 1985).

at the institute for Humanities in Africa (HUMA) and the University of California in Davis. More importantly, Ayanda is a kind, generous and thoughtful human being, and my mentor through the Mellon Mays Undergraduate Fellowship and beyond. On the first walk he had suggested that I read the work of Rob Morrell, one of the foremost academics in the burgeoning field of Critical Studies of Men and Masculinities. Years later, Morrell's work has left an indelible mark on this book and my trajectory in academia. When I reached out to him to write the preface for this book at the advice of Professor Francis Nyamnjoh, Dr. Morrell politely accepted and requested that we meet for coffee. When we met, he asked why I was doing work on masculinities. Like him, I had been physically bullied growing up, and was trying to make sense of masculine dynamics in my life, possibly to reclaim some of the robbed agency in what was a confusing stage of my childhood and adolescence. We discussed pain and its visceral aftereffects, and gratitude in having found a sense of fulfilment through the academic project in processing some of that pain. "Why Upington?", he wanted to know. Again, we return to Ayanda. I told him of my experiences on holidays in my mom's hometown, and he expressed a real interest in my elaboration of some of the masculine dynamics in Upington. This was a big town that had made me and so many of my family and friends but received little attention from South African social scientists in relation to urban hubs like Cape Town and Johannesburg.

Contemporary academic literature on masculinities in Upington is lacking, and popular media presents a one-tracked and rather gloomy narrative on men in the region. Upington has been growing consistently since the 1930's, influenced by its position as an urban hub for the many farm regions around it in the central Northern Cape which could not adequately support young Black men who took to the town to find work (Breckenridge, 1998). This was the case for my mother's family too. Nearly a century later, the town and its people suffer from large-scale unemployment, frequent drug abuse, coupled with the other mechanisms for coping in a harsh physical environment (See Chapter 4 for more details on responses to these conditions). Upington is also no stranger to the racialised histories of Apartheid and its spatial planning, which influence the ways in which permissible masculinities are imagined (Brown, 2012; Salo, 2010). Life is continuously being made, however, and community initiatives reflect the belief in Upington as a viable place to raise new life and thrive for current generations (News24.com, 2024). In Upington, teenage alcohol abuse is rife, as is crime and often-fatal stabbings, most perpetrators of which are men (Ofm.co.za, 2024). These news articles, represent an incomplete version of the real happenings and masculinity formations in the town, often prioritising sensationalised and pessimistic narratives. Located on the banks of the Orange River, Upington is capable of breathtaking beauty, and hosts a tight-knit community where you could recognise anyone at any time. I wanted to find out how sports clubs in this town influenced the ways in which masculinities were being spoken about, and find the stories that were hidden behind the totalising story of drugs, alcohol and gender-based violence, while being open to hearing the harsh realities of lived experience and structural oppression that plays out on a daily basis. I wanted to know about complexities and what made men in this town. I returned to the Northern Cape.

Setting the Scene: Upington and Unavoidable Subjectivities

The baking sun held me in its inescapable, stifling stare. Each year my footprints left larger marks in the red sand, as I dragged my suitcase from the car into my Aunt and Uncle's home. The sweat, freely flowing down my face, represented liberation. Summer holidays! I was spending it in Upington. My mom was born and raised in Upington, and it was here that she met my father. He was from Cape Town and had moved to Upington to pursue teaching in a new phase of his life. This town, hosting about 75 000 people in the heart of South Africa's least populous province, is not my definition of a typical holiday destination. For one, the sand was red, and not white. The beach was substituted by inflatable plastic pools that would scald you if you lingered against the rim for too long. The sunshine was brutal. Our national sports teams never felt the need to stop here - probably because of the aforementioned oppressive sun. And yet my heart was filled with joy. I would pinch myself in excitement, eagerly anticipating the next few weeks of freedom, hanging out with my cousins, and eating some of the best curries, salads and *braaivleis*[3] on offer. The people made Upington the perfect holiday destination. This time I arrived with a notepad in hand, ready to interrogate questions about masculinities while building new relationships with town residents (See Chapter 2).

---

[3] Meats prepared on the open fire.

A large part of the justification for this chapter and its particularly storied nature, is addressing the subjective influence of the researcher on the research. The tradition of fieldnotes and its manifestation through ethnography typically set Anthropologists apart as distinct amongst social scientists (Sanjek, 1990). Geertz' (1973) intervention in the theory of fieldwork highlighted the Anthropologists' role as an interpreter as well as a describer, concerned with the minute details that manifest a wide array of social meaning and cultural ideas. Being trained in the tradition of Anthropology, my note-taking resembled that of many others who are eager to leave the field with tangible messages from themselves in the moment. I had a notepad filled with fieldnotes. Some were barely legible. Others were poetic and descriptive. These fieldnotes are not what you will read in this book, however. Headnotes are the thoughts and memories which are embodied in the researcher (Sanjek, 1990). Headnotes are shaped by encounters in the field that leave lasting impressions (Sanjek, 1990).

> [The Anthropologist] comes back from the field with fieldnotes and headnotes. The fieldnotes stay the same, written down on paper, but the headnotes continue to evolve and change as they did during the time in the field (Sanjek, 1990:93).

Ethnography is a product of the divergence of the two, with the headnotes taking priority in the produced narratives. The characters encountered in the work are nuanced and shaped by the perspectives of the researcher (Mead, 1977). This does not mean the researcher should have a heightened sense of self-importance. Rather, there should be increased humility, with the possibility of getting it wrong or claiming damaging, colonial notions of elusive objectivity always on the horizon (Pratt, 1992). I attempt, in this chapter, to provide context to the journey to the field, and the need to be open to the emergence and continually evolving interpretations of the encounters I witnessed.

The emergence of the headnotes points towards a need for attentively practicing reflexivity in presenting research. Francis Nyamnjoh (2012) highlights the failings of many a researcher in studying others to pay attention to their own lived experiences and unstated assumptions in producing seemingly objective work about the "other". He (2012) argues for a need to acknowledge and reflect on the worlds and power dynamics which underly Anthropological evaluation. In this work, I am both the researcher and a member of the researched at various levels, with my own input and inherited biases influencing what I deem noteworthy in the field. Attempting to a reflexivity that extends beyond "lip-service" or a basic description of positionality, I share, within reason, some of the experiences that led me to the field. This is an attempt at tracing parts of my histories how they continue to influence and shape the dissemination of my observations, which, although honest, may not always be true to the experiences of others who observe or make up the field (Nyamnjoh, 2012). I have, however, tried to prioritise the stories shared by the participants in this work. I am open to revelations of missed key areas of masculinities and its manifestation in Upington sports clubs. Sharing some of my lived experiences and biased views from the romanticising, storytelling elements of my persona may help the reader recognise how I came to describe the field in certain ways, and why this project held so much at stake for making sense of my worlds as well as the worlds of those whom I built relationships with in 2023. I hope it does justice to the complex lives of the participants, and the wide emergence of post-colonial identity formations in Africa.

Gender and Belonging

In Upington, I was embedded in layers of belonging, negotiating it differently in different situations. I was born in the town. I had family members in most areas and could navigate on foot with relative ease. On the other hand, I knew very few sportsmen, my Afrikaans – the dominant language in the town – requires significant work, and I had never lived there indefinitely. I also remember writing a particularly cringeworthy essay in high school about the "simple lives of my cousins up North". I was a boy from the city, and a foolish and naïve one at that, buying into town-mouse and country-mouse delusions of superiority. I also remember the visceral feeling of freedom and joy whenever my household would make the road trip to Upington for almost every school holiday, and the joy of carrying bags into the house and playing with my cousins.

Growing up, gender never seemed to be a complicated category of being. I knew that I was a boy. I knew I loved sports, and that this pastime pleased me and many other boys around me. An impromptu game of soccer was never that far away in homosocial contexts. In any given organisation of people, there exists patterns of gender dynamics labelled by Connell (2006:839) as "a gender regime", where the division of labour, power, emotion and interconnectivity, and symbolism are implicitly and explicitly gendered. I was subjected to gender regimes in Cape Town, at home, church and school most obviously. In Upington, however, I seemed to notice the gender regime in less tactful ways. I would be expected to help carry equipment and fix objects around the house. My girl cousins and sister would be expected to help in the kitchen. While play was less explicitly divided, games of rugby would be considered "boys-only" while unironically playing with a barbie doll in hand would mean a form of social self-harm. We would groan at the suggestion of watching a "chick flick" and celebrate when my uncle switched the TV to the football. Most egregiously, I remember being served food with the men (despite my status as a member of the generation of children), while my older adult girl cousins[4] were served last, after the children. I ate the food guiltily amidst glares from my cousins who had expected me to protest the unfairness of the moment. I would take their stares over challenging the decrees of my aunts.

It was in Upington that I excitedly played with my three favourite girl cousins. Their ages all fell within two years of mine. At age seven, somewhat unconscious of the taboos of acting out of character with my gender, I was fascinated by the makeup routines and fashion shows my cousins seemed to dream up every day that holiday. Noticing my interest, they decided that they had found a new model to experiment on. I obliged. I loved the attention. I remember feeling silly, almost twisting my ankle in my older cousin's high heels. This was a hoot! I could barely contain my giggles as I was introduced to the aunts and uncles sitting on the couches in the spacious living room. When I entered, I was the only one smiling. My Aunt Susan (a family friend) looked

[4] One of whom had two children by this point.

crestfallen and swooped up to collect me. The heels stayed behind. I was promptly asked if I knew I was a boy and that I was not to dress up in clothing meant for girls. This, I reasoned, was an unnecessary line of questioning. Why wasn't everybody sharing the joke? The significance behind why my family did not share my humorous take on the fashion show became clearer only years later (See Chapter 5 for a more specific focus on Black masculinities and its intersection with sexualities in Upington).

I knew I was a sensitive boy growing up. This greatly angered me. Why was it that every time I became angry, frustrated or dejected, it manifested in tears? I was also particularly conniving, smart-mouthed and resentful. I was not the easiest child to get along with, or to raise, I imagine. As I began emerging into my teen years, I began enjoying socialisation a whole lot more than I had during my childhood. While I still enjoyed being a recluse and remained terribly shy, I really enjoyed engaging discussion, positive attention and adulation that often accompanied observing the most attractive behaviour to whomever I perceived to be the most influential person in the room. Even better if this performance of agreeableness actually aligned with my values[5]. In some situations, the expected portrayal of masculinity did not align with what I was feeling. Sometimes, I wanted to cry. Sometimes, I wanted to be silly and show how excited I was to be with a group of my peers, watching sports or even just discussing pretty girls. I knew that these outbursts of emotion were not manly. Additionally, I was never a particularly

[5] These values were very much in flux at the time, and I still operate with a great degree of openness and naivety. I do struggle to voice my opinion at times, not wanting to incite confrontation unless absolutely necessary.

incredible physical specimen - although I knew my way around a cricket ball. I was beat up quite a few times growing up, by older boys and men. Many times, my "smart" mouth and defiant attitude got me into these situations, and I never seemed to throw so much as a punch to defend myself, responding only with the most malicious words that my enraged mind could conjure. A big part of me needed, and still needs, to attempt a better understanding at this "being a man" thing. The rules seemed to change, and while many times I really enjoyed these performances, I sometimes felt short-changed by social expectation, and hurt by the inability to sit down and discuss gendered pain with other men (See Chapter 7 for an explicit focus on sharing and affective health).

Concluding the Start: Motivating Factors and Justifications for Research

These personal anecdotes were slightly more vulnerable than I had intended. Additionally, I ask, as you may have done paragraphs ago: "so what?" I believe these stories were necessary inclusions. Choosing a topic for my research was not arbitrary. While I knew that studying masculinities would be an attractive proposition in terms of relatability and access to research participants, there is a big part of me that needed to take up this quest. This ethnography was not thought up as a quest for healing[6], but as a quest for sense-making. The two,

---

[6] I remember humorously, the comment made by Dr. Lerato Mokwena – a foremost researcher on the Northern Cape – at a recent Mellon event that we (emerging graduate students) should go to therapy, and not look for healing and solace in our research. While I agree with her comment, I think a healthy

however, seem intertwined in my more recent thinking. Telling you a little bit more about Upington, the gendered experiences that stand out to me and my attempts at understanding my identity growing up, have given you the basis for why I operate with the methodology you will read about in the next chapter. This project is as personal as it is professional. I cannot leave myself at the door. I hope that, as you read, it resonates with your own sense of being in the world. I want to add to an archive which prioritises Upington, and the wider Northern Cape as a valid area of Anthropological research. It is the people that matter the most. More than that, I want this work to build towards more fruitful and measured understandings of youth, masculinities and sports clubs, and the exciting possibilities embedded beneath the seemingly dominant stories of unarticulated pain, delinquency and violence. I envision a romanticised world where attending to intersectionality pushes us to prioritise understanding and love, over judgment, selfishness and reproduced pain.

This introductory chapter is an attempt to preface the justifications for this work and show you how I think through my own place as a researcher and incomplete curator of these narratives. This chapter is followed by an exploration of the research methodologies employed in this work which will also highlight the research questions which animate this project. It will then follow a review of the most relevant literature to answer and fuel initial questions into the field and highlight critical gaps in the existing archive. The next chapter is the first of four chapters

---

attachment and personal motivation to research is commonplace in academia, and should be acknowledged for its capacities and flaws.

which analyse the data gathered in the field. It focuses on the construction of men in relation to responsibilities, and the nuances of these responsibilities and ideas of masculine success across the sports club. Secondly, an intersectional lens is used to evaluate the complexities of race, class, sexuality and ableism in the discourse and shaping of permissible ways of being a man in the sports club. The penultimate data analysis chapter is concerned with touch and rituals in the sports club, culminating in narratives of masculinities and loyalty to sports and the sports club in the aftermath of death and its constant possibility. Finally, the data analysis in this book concludes with an overview of discussions of affective masculine health, and the role of religion, mentorship and the idea of the club as a family in regulating affect. This work is a necessary, and incomplete addition to important conversations around masculinities through the structures which shape its performances in different contexts. It also contributes to a much-needed archive on social dynamics and ways of being in the Northern Cape and more specifically Upington, whose people never cease to amaze me with their graciousness and lessons for life.

Chapter 2

"Back Home": The Man, the Empty Field and the Notepad

Introduction

My research was inspired by a central overarching question, namely: How do sports clubs influence conceptions, embodiment and performances of masculinities amongst young men in Upington in the Northern Cape, South Africa?

To answer this research question, I needed to work with sports clubs in Upington. I was eager to meet its members, the target group of men who would assist me in answering this question. I remembered from my own time as a member of a football club, that while it was often easy for me to get a conversation going about sports, discussing the love for sports or its effects on the players and coaches and their masculine identities was a conversation rarely broached. This was one of the motivating themes this research sought to address, with particular focus on the social structure of the sports club. Which clubs would I find, and who would consent to having an Anthropologist (albeit a budding one) watch their every move from the sidelines, taking notes about their lived experiences without fully understanding the complexity of relationships and experiences that had manifested in the moments I would observe – "stealing" them from their context to make ethnographic sense?

Conceptual Framework

This would lead me to a conceptual framework that would motivate my steps into the field to begin with – incompleteness. Francis Nyamnjoh (2017) argues that lived experiences are incomplete, and that conviviality is a tool for acknowledging incompleteness through activation with incomplete others. These encounters do not produce completeness, but allow for nuanced learning which avoid claims to completeness and violent coercion that often follow such claims. "Full understandings of the complexity of relationships and experiences" escapes even the most deeply involved members, because the moment that one decides something has been understood, the person is closed off from receiving new information, deviations from stability and deeper complexity – or perhaps shallower simplicities (Nyamnjoh, 2017). The "friction" of encounters, with its messy and often awkward components was a reminder to avoid errant universal discourses about sports clubs, men and Upington that would leave these categories reified, with no room to acknowledge their movements and flows outside of a rigid structure (Tsing, 2005:4). This work is messy. It is in tune with the mess of real life encounters and relationships that shape and are shaped by people and the multiplicity of quests that drive them daily. I could not even begin to do honest and worthwhile work without having encounters with the people I would write about (Tsing, 2005). The research question will be attended to by the revelation of stories and experiences from the members of the sports clubs, and myself as an observer - negotiating his inclusion at various levels of social intimacy. It would be foolish to claim to present a complete or final product about masculinities in Upington sports clubs. Now that I had been freed from that pressure, I could go about my fieldwork recognizing myself as an incomplete and necessary traveller through a mobile space, sharing stories that hopefully contribute towards a more nuanced understanding of the influence of sports clubs on its members, young men in Upington.

Finding the Field

To investigate the research question, I had made the 14-hour bus voyage to the town of my birth. Returning to Upington has always been joyous for me. This time, the joy was accompanied by trepidation. I would stay there for two periods across 7 weeks (18 January – 5 February 2023, and 4 June – 10 July 2023). Smackbang in the middle of the Kalahari desert, I was encompassed by the inescapable summer heat. I had sent out emails to various clubs in the region, across the "big three" team sports of football, rugby and cricket, assuming that their popularity meant these clubs would be easily accessible. There was no reply. Conversations with my family during the preceding holidays however, had left me with enthusiasm that these connections could be made in person, utilizing their webs of contact. My Uncle and Aunt were gracious hosts and particularly active and well-known in the town. All their children had played sports at a high level and my Uncle was a rugby coach and football administrator for his own grassroots club. Their home would be a superbly hospitable temporary home for me as I navigated my research period.

During the first stay, in late January, I made initial connections with the clubs I would work with. I remember running an errand for my Aunt at the mall, wondering how to find an entry point into conducting this research. Formal bureaucratic enquiries had failed. As I left the mall, I quickly doubled back. Had I seen correctly? It was midday and an adjacent field on the premises of the local Further Education and Training (FET) college, was filled with players in fully sponsored gear, doing stretches and light activities with footballs. I stumbled onto the pitch and secured permission to return the following day, outlining my proposal to the coach and technical director. My research had begun. The club's name was Upington City Football Club. They were semi-professional, with aspirations of soon playing in the Premier Soccer League at the highest tier of South African Football. Training on the very same field as Upington City, albeit three times per week and in the evenings, was an amateur rugby club I had become aware of through my cousin's partner. He was a player there. The day after I met Upington City, he procured permission from the coach on my behalf, for me to present my proposal and observe and interview players at their club. This club was the Defence Force Collegiates Rugby Club, or DFC. In the space of two days, the anthropological field had allowed me in through a football and rugby club playing on the very same sports field!

Playing (With) Anthropology

Methods

I entered the field with three proposed Anthropological methods: ethnography, participant observation and interviews. The former would be my method of data translation and packaging into what I hope is a potent and meaningful story about the social zones negotiated during my time in the field. The latter methods were data collection tools.

Participant Observation

Participant observation (Russel, 2006; Geertz, 1973) was the main tool I used during club training sessions, often sitting on the bleachers with a notebook on my lap, or walking nearby action zones on the field. Both clubs' management teams had provided consent for me to observe - not trifling with play itself was an unwritten rule I wanted to abide by so as not to take away from the club's sporting objectives. On a personal front, I wanted to avoid annoying my new acquaintances. I directly observed at Upington City for approximately ten training sessions, while sitting on the bleachers for fifteen of DFC's evening sessions. These observations were focused on performances of embodied masculinities. I was also intrigued by the different sites of sociality and masculine influence. The team huddle - where I found myself interlocking arms with the exhausted, heavily-breathing players as a recognized part - which took place at the end of practice, was a different zone of negotiating masculinities from the field of play, the carpools home, and the bleachers on which the players changed kit. Recognizing these different sites of masculine influence will help avoid singular narratives about hegemonic masculinity currently present in Critical Studies and Masculinities (Connell, 2005; Morrell, 2012; Ratele, 2016). Participant observation allowed me to get a sensory and tactile understanding of the playing out of masculinities in the field beyond secondary data like interviews (Russel, 2006). It allowed me to gain familiarity with the processes involved in the social aspect of sports clubs and more personal familiarity with the players, who began to recognize me as a part of practice with my own special duty.

Formal Interviews

Interviews became an essential mode of data collection at Upington City in January. After practice, I would ride along in the team bus as we made our way to the clubhouse. At the conclusion of games of Ludo, I approached senior players and interviewed them about their time at the club, their understanding of their own masculinities and their motivations and aspirations within the space. These interviews ranged in length, with some establishing a deep connection and personal conversations in which participants and I shared anecdotes about our lives. I saw these rich interview encounters as the manifestation of a call from one of the coaches, urging the players to work with me in order to "better understand ourselves as men". I was struck by the willingness of Upington City's players to talk, often "booking" the next interview slot. In complete contrast, I undertook no formal interviews with DFC players in the first research period, being gently rejected. I understood this difference to be attributed to the time of practice - DFC meeting in the evenings after workdays, while Upington City players trained in the morning, were paid by the club and generally had more downtime. In addition, I may have been seen as a member of the media that usually accompanies footballing progression, a symbol of activation into a realm of stardom. Regardless of the motives, I was happy to have willing participants. At DFC, I needed to engage in informal interviews and get to know players through mobile phone exchanges before setting up formal interviews. In total, I formally interviewed six football players, three rugby players, interviewing each head coach, respectively.

Conversations

Even more important to learning club member perspectives however, were informal conversations. These conversations helped humanize the "research participants" as fellow men, negotiating what it means to be a man. Gaining player perspectives, wrapped up in intersectional identities will hopefully allow an analysis that goes deeper than ineffective "Masculinities in Crisis"[7] theories that have littered popular media on the social category (Musariri, 2021). Through these conversations most tangibly, belonging and insiderness was negotiated, most often through discussions of recent sporting activity and complaining about the weather - burning and freezing together, the open bleachers providing little shelter from the elements. Insights were exchanged reciprocally and relationships were built. These conversations also allowed me to peer into the histories of the club and provide vital contexts for the stories shared in this book. Some players did not want to be formally interviewed, and the informal conversations allowed me to learn from them while navigating more comfortable terrain.

---

[7] These theories typically characterize a "traditional" masculinity – the misogynistic, violent, sexually driven man – with its power under threat having failed to adapt to the legal, social and institutional changes ushered in by democracy, responding with violence towards women, queer groups and non-hegemonic masculinities (Morrell, 1998, Jewkes et. al., 2010).

Positionality, Belonging and Reflexivity

My methods all had a distinctly personal element to them, a presence that often characterizes Anthropology. The researcher enters the field with all their "personal baggage, assumptions, beliefs" and prior perspectives of the field, the people they meet there and the research question (Behar, 1996:8). My methods for employing research were based heavily on my positionality. As a student of Anthropology, I was encouraged to pursue deep immersion in the field (Geertz, 1973:7), thickly describing my experiences and inviting club members to conversations around the research question. The questions I asked and the notes I took were filtered around what I considered noteworthy, and therefore it is important to attempt to do justice to reflexivity in the field (Nyamnjoh, 2012). I was also researching in Upington, my hometown, with the people with whom I shared certain aspirations, affinities and values. This book will attempt to locate my positionality within the club structure and in relation to those around me.

Belonging and insiderness was a facet of the research that intimidated me. I had been born in Upington, but I lived in Cape Town. I knew one club member prior to my entry to the field. Just because I had been born there, however, did not entitle me to a sense of belonging often loosely attributed to a "native Anthropologist" (Narayan, 1993). Belonging, in any case, was negotiated within zones of sociality (Nyamnjoh, 2016), and not a permanent attribute to be attained through a single negotiation. I entered into the field negotiating various layers of insider and outsider status. Acknowledging and reflecting on my positionality in the field has two explicit purposes in this work. Firstly, it is important to attempt an understanding of my own lenses and offerings that arise from my position as different to the group of players. For example, Black Feminist scholar, Patricia Collins (1986:516) argues that outsider status within groups can allow group members to confide in the stranger - a benefit that played out in the heavily personal interviews. It is also beneficial for recognizing patterns not as easily visible to those immersed therein. Secondly, it seeks to avoid replicating a sense of detached objectivity present in the colonial tradition of the Malinowski's, in which the discipline of Anthropology has its formal birth. I am a person negotiating his own masculinity. I am not a blank canvas in my observations, and this will be reflected as I speak about my own experiences at the sports clubs.

The Notepad

Throughout my observation period I carried a notepad in my bag. Here I would jot down observations, possible interview questions, and some of my own feelings during practice sessions. This notepad became both my sign of difference and totem of inclusion. The coach made a point of emphasizing the phrase "doen jou werk (do your work)", in team huddles. The marker of a bad teammate, I was told, was not knowing your responsibilities. That made you a freeloader. The notepad represented my role as an Anthropologist in the space. The players knew I was observing them. While they wore rugby boots and athletic clothing, I had my notepad. This pointed marker of difference was addressed explicitly when Carlton, a player who had not been at the training sessions I attended, approached me on a match day. "Sorry to disturb boss", he said, tapping me on the shoulder, "but what do you do with that notepad?" My role as an Anthropologist was explained. I was not a rugby player, but I was not merely a spectator or close kin with the players either. I had adopted a distinct role in the social web of the club, as the one whose work is to listen, talk and jot and not play. The notepad helped acknowledge my difference while providing a sense of inclusion in the wider squad - and provided the opportunity for me to share the project with curious players.

The Empty Field

One of the struggles I found upon my return in June, was that the football season had come to a climax, with Upington City playing in a playoff tournament in Pietermaritzburg, far away from Upington. I had no family there. My study was not based there. This was a major oversight on my behalf. In February, I had received permission to continue my work there in June, with management acknowledging it as the final month of the football season. Leading up to my return, I had messaged the club's physiotherapist, a gracious host who had been my primary point of contact with the club during the first research period. My messages did not get through. An attempt at contacting the club through their Instagram page also yielded no fruit. Instead of doing due diligence to establish contact through travel or an acquaintance in the town, I foolishly trusted that the club would be in operation when I returned in June. The gates to the clubhouse were locked. The training field was empty.

DFC - who were in full swing - became the main focus of my June research. I was concerned but not distraught, as February had yielded a surprising trove of data given my intention to only establish primary contact. The result however, is a recency and perhaps data volume bias towards DFC. Future studies in the region would benefit from multiple sources of contact to the sports clubs, and a more comprehensive anticipation of the schedules within the sports' structures. In addition, I believe future studies on the effects of sports clubs on masculinities in the region would benefit from a specialised look across different sports clubs within the same sport, asking perhaps more specific questions about masculinities across different settings in the same game. For example, is there something unique to the dynamics of rugby clubs in Upington, a cultural practice or embodiment of masculinity that can be attributed to specific practices in the sport such as scrums? The field of sports club has much to offer Gender Studies, Anthropologists and anyone eager to gain a deeper understanding of the influences of behaviour and understandings within these influential milieus.

Ethics

All the observation research I undertook in this project was pre-arranged through informed verbal consent with the management teams of DFC and Upington City respectively, both of whom invited me to matches. All research participants had full legal capacity to provide informed consent. This coincides with Upington's Amateur Rugby League rules, and Upington City's contractual policy, which does not allow minors to participate as full club members.

Every person that was formally interviewed gave consent to use the data I received from them for the purposes of the project which was explained to them in accordance with Anthropology Southern Africa's appeal for overt scholarship and interlocutor consent (Anthropology Southern Africa, 2004). Where possible, this book commits to anonymity in player interactions, using pseudonyms so as not to cause undue stress related to revealed identities. It will, however, use the names of the coaches, which would be impossible to hide anyway, given the publicly accessible nature of the role, and the fact that the real names of the clubs are used. I am committed to my own personal integrity, and this book will commit to an honest account of my experiences. I recognize that these experiences may be subjective. On occasions where I overheard potentially derogatory remarks, I avoided broaching the subject for fear of closing off further research, building barriers through personal judgement. The presence of such remarks will be omitted or included in the research according to its necessity towards understanding the research question. I am an Anthropologist and human with my own flaws, not an arbiter of righteousness.

Finally, English was the most common medium through which I spoke to participants, although I received a significant amount of data in Afrikaans, the dominant language in Upington in which I am fluent. Upington City had a wider variety of languages which made up conversations in training, including isiZulu, isiXhosa and Sotho. I would like to thank many of my interlocutors for accommodating my language limitations and answering my interview questions in English. On occasion, a player struggled to convey a message using a words not directly translatable to English. This book will, however, strongly attempt to do justice to the stories, messages and understandings of the participants – all of whom were gracious in allowing me to infringe on their time. This book will also utilize a more dynamic form of writing in an attempt to make it more accessible to wider audiences and not exclusively academic – while still acknowledging that this book is academic and must adhere to its rigors. The results of this research, will hopefully contribute to a better understanding of the sociality in Upington's sports clubs and its effects on men in the region, and South Africa as a whole. This research has a personal element to me as a man passionate about sports institutions and sport as a foundational leisure activity for myself and many others. It is an attempt to add to a series of debates and competing knowledge systems that will hopefully lead to a decolonial future and more inclusivity and nuanced awareness of gender performance in Upington, a town dear to me.

Chapter 3

Literature Review: "Masculinities And Sports Clubs"

Introduction

This review will begin with a brief overview of key works on gender that have inspired the frameworks and literature used in this book, arguing for the importance of this work and the social negotiation of gender. It will then separate the research question into four literature discussions. The first is a discussion of emerging arguments in Critical Studies of Men and Masculinities. This literature, particularly from a South African lens, exposes the one-sided nature of public and academic discourses on hegemonic masculinity and reveals the need for more nuanced, intersectional scholarship on masculinities, acknowledging the histories and diverse experience of different groups in the country. The second section presents a brief history of sports clubs in South Africa, highlighting its use to regulate the leisure time of Black men and its import for establishing masculine status. The next discussion highlights the impact of sports clubs on the masculine body through trained techniques and machination. Finally, it will conclude with a discussion from development discourses and work done on masculine archetypes in sports clubs, framing masculine ideals towards a disciplined, skilful and moral body and its importance in gaining prestige from other men. Altogether, this review will argue for the need to examine sports clubs as both agents and vectors for masculine activation and more specificity in engaging with intersections of identity in Critical Studies of Men and Masculinities.

Overarching Gender Literature and Framework

Masculinities have received increased academic attention in the past 25 years, and are a contentious topic in popular South African media. One of the major contributors to this increase in academic attention was Judith Butler's (2003) "*Performative Acts and Gender Constitution*", a seminal text for feminist theories on gender. She presents gender as a constantly negotiated sum of a series of performative acts, as opposed to being a fixed identity marker out of which one acts (2003:98). Gender is not arbitrary, however. Gender has very real implications for what is permissible within shifting cultural boundaries (Oyewumi, 1997:81). The inherited stories and gendered traditions are not at the whims of a completely independent agent - people are bound by regulations which delineate the limits of conceptions of gender (1997:83). Gender is shaped by and influences sociality, the body and interactions. Gender matters. The sports club, therefore, will provide a critical lens into how young men in Upington conceptualise and practice masculinities through club participation. If personal agency is bordered by social frameworks and repeated practices of gender, then for athletes, sports clubs serve as a frontier where these understandings may be debated, contested or reinforced (Kovač, 2021). How do club structures expand or narrow masculine practices? What is its role in regulating the social constructions and conceptualisations of masculinities in Upington? I am particularly interested in addressing these questions through the lens of my fieldwork experiences.

The Man in the Canon

Popular media about men and masculinities have tended to adopt a singular framework in South Africa, particularly in conversations on the social media platform, Twitter, and with reason. Gender-based violence is at an all-time high (Musariri, 2021:889). Masculinity has often been described as "in crisis"[8] in the South African context (Musariri, 2021:890). Discussions on hegemonic masculinity frequently revolve around violence and power exerted over "subordinate" masculinities, queer groups and women. Contestations between masculinities often result in violence (Ratele, 2015). Physical prowess serves as an ideal for many boys, even at the primary school level and before, partly for the use of aggression and efficiency at sports (Bhana, 2008:3). The concept of a single hegemonic masculinity does not translate well to the South African context (Morrell, Jewkes & Lindegger, 2012:14). Masculinities, like many mobilized categories in life, cannot be effectively grappled with and understood when separated from their context. Key theorist on masculinities in South Africa, Robert Morrell (2012:12), argues that masculinities must be located in the fractal racial and class-based realities of

---

[8] These theories typically characterize a "traditional" masculinity – the misogynistic, violent, sexually driven man – with its power under threat having failed to adapt to the legal, social and institutional changes ushered in by democracy, responding with violence towards women, queer groups and non-hegemonic masculinities (Morrell, 1998, Jewkes et. al., 2010).

the post-colonial South African State. Hegemonic masculinities, therefore, present differently according to locations, racial histories and a plethora of other intersections and categories.

This research aims to respond to a call for more nuanced, intersectional research in the Critical Studies of Men and Masculinities (Ratele, 2015:144 & Mfecane, 2020:3). Both Morrell and Kopano Ratele (2016) - a psychologist and important figure in men's studies in South Africa - agree that post-Apartheid conceptions of masculinity respond to histories of discrimination. Both agree on the concept of a white hegemonic masculinity - based on financial and institutional power (Morrell, et.al. 2012:12). Both also agree on a Black hegemonic masculinity - where Blackness is deemed a product of shared social experience and historical oppression in South Africa (Ratele, 2016:1). Black hegemonic masculinities are understood to be shaped by urban migration and displacement, and manifest in problematic practices of substance abuse, risky sexual behaviour and domestic violence (Morrell, et.al., 2012:13). More nuance is needed in these framings of dominant masculinities in South Africa. For example, how do coloured young men in Upington understand the dominant gender dynamics in the club and other social zones in the region? My work will attempt to add to and enrich an important canon in understanding masculinities in Upington, South Africa, Africa and the world.

South African Sports Clubs

A brief history of sports clubs and its uses, aims and motivations in colonial Africa will benefit this research by framing its importance for the formation of masculine identities in the region. Anthropology has frequently fallen short on taking play as seriously as work - often assuming definite separation between the two and rendering the former as "low-stakes" social interaction (Malaby, 2009). Anyone who has watched rugby matches in South Africa would laugh at a low-stakes summary of the activities they witness. Formal sports clubs have colonial legacies in 19th century Southern Africa, especially the introduction of Cricket, Soccer and Rugby - all sports originating in England (Coetzee, et.al, 2021). As part of colonial expansion, the British used sports clubs to re-establish the authority of English as a medium of instruction and as a site for the exchange of moral codes and social attitudes (Nauright, 1998). Pre-colonial sports and games - although this taxonomy is incomplete - existed. These were largely written out of Western historiographies and blurred lines between work and leisure, such as bow-shooting, wrestling and Assegai throwing (Keimbou, 2005). Like many sports, and processes of integration into sports clubs, these served as rites of passage for many young boys negotiating social acceptance into manhood (2005:454). Encounters between colonial administrators and African people saw an incorporation of the rules of the British games to the African colonial context.

Colonial administrators saw sports clubs as a means of distraction for young men who were deemed dangerous if idle. Part of colonial control and Apartheid planning was to "moralize the leisure time of Black Africans" and men in particular (Nauright, 1998:71). Sports were regarded as the "proper" activity for men outside of work (Nauright, 1998:70). For many men, belonging to sports clubs was, and still is, a fundamental part of constructing their own masculinities and identities as men. Meaning is mobilized and status is negotiated through ritual games such as sports, and through the clubs that serve as its vectors at an organized level (Malaby, 2009: 214). In essence, South African sports are by no means low-stakes.

The Masculine Body

Important Anthropological literature on the intersections between sports clubs and masculinities are centred around uses of the body as a machine. Marcell Mauss (1973), in *Techniques of the body,* argues that for masculinities heavily constructed around sporting cultures, the body is not a completely arbitrary biological fact. Understanding the body is important to understanding the world that organizes it (Kembou, 2005:453). The masculine body is shaped by gender performance. It is regulated through culturally specific teaching practices and social norms (Mauss, 1973:71) through which gender is affirmed and practiced (Butler, 2003:98). The education which young men receive at sports clubs hone the bodily techniques they practice, often based on close imitation of other men they deem to be more successful within the sport, club structure or the arena of life in general (Mauss, 1973:75). The body is proposed as a machine that can be improved upon through training, developing into a more effective tool for success on the sports field.

Discipline is a value that is essential for such mechanistic views of the masculine body. Mauss (1973:78) argues that men voluntarily submit themselves to training in order to discipline the body as an effective tool for success. This is not to say that all men subscribe to Mauss' description of the disciplined regimes of the club, but they are often – especially in the case of youth clubs – strongly encouraged to. Success at sports becomes an important tool for gaining cultural capital as a man. Discipline is therefore one of the embodied ideals that is deemed fundamental to the shaping of masculinities, to benefit both the sports club by winning, and the individual through winning's collateral rewards.

Ideal over Idle

The South African State's development narrative around sports clubs has its own ideals for sports clubs and men. These ideals often address conditions of precarity, especially in urban townships, offering an antidote to the "problem" of the idle man. Sponsorship is invested to sports clubs on a two-fold expected return. Firstly, the club pushes its most talented members towards potential activation through professional sports and the lucrative stardom it offers - in a rags-to-riches story of material success (Bogopa, 2001). For the members who do not have what it takes to make a living out of sports, the club still serves as a way to keep them off the streets and away from criminal activity or harmful vices, especially juvenile delinquency (Bogopa, 2001). This framing represents masculinities as dangerous to the state when they are idle. The problem of the idle man is reflected in the moralizing mission of the sports club. Uroš Kovač (2021), an emerging anthropologist in masculinities studies agrees that sports clubs are a moral agent for young African men belonging to sports clubs. He did research on masculine identities through football in Cameroon in a similar moment to my own research. His findings show how gendered subjects are shaped by club structures and socialities according to moral judgements about what it means to be a man, especially in precarious conditions (2021:80).

The sports club serves as a host and simultaneous agent for producing moral subjects by encouraging certain tropes and gendered habits and presenting them in contrast to less favourable masculine stereotypes. For example, the two footballing identities presented by Kovač in Beau, Cameroon represent polar opposites and different paths for social activation in and around the club. A popular type of footballing masculinity is the "bad boy", who parties lavishly, spends money, and is considered a womanizer[9] who lacks discipline (Kovač, 2021:80). The bad boy is often strongly discouraged by the club management. While the bad boy is activated by certain social sections of the club and is often popular, some have been expelled from their clubs because of reckless behaviour – especially at the highest level of sports[10] (Mfecane, 2018:299). The opposite trope, the "disciplined", "humble", "monogamous", "God-fearing" and "sober" man, is typically encouraged by clubs, moralizing agents towards a masculinity that could offer the member a better chance at opportunities for ascension to material activation in professional sports, or deeper involvement and higher status at their current clubs (Kovač, 2021:80).

For young men especially, social activation into new responsibilities and benefits is achieved through

---

[9] This particular phrasing implies not only engagement with multiple sexual partners, but has a heterosexual framing.

[10] See Adrian Mutu, Jabu Mahlangu and even recently the global superstar Cristiano Ronaldo at Manchester United as examples.

consensus with their peers and elders, often at the club (Fuh, 2012:503). Prestige economies refer to the ways in which young men negotiate status and win respect of other men in order to activate more tangible rewards in the face of precarity (Fuh, 2012). The Sports club, therefore, serves as a host and agent of morality and prestige economies. While most masculinities are in operation somewhere between the extremes of the two tropes, what is revealed are masculine ideals for members to aim at, with its associated benefits and sacrifices.

Conclusion

Anthropological sources on sports clubs and masculinities converge on an ideal to be aspired towards, a masculine ideal of body, discipline and morality. This book will examine some of the ideals and masculinities encouraged in Upington sports clubs through conversation and imitated action. How are these ideas discussed and embodied? What are the correlations and departures between the two, and what are the nuances overshadowed in the current Anthropological canon? While serving as a vector for exchanged ideas on morality, admired masculinities and discipline, I am intrigued by how the sports club incorporates the dreams, careers and leisure of its members – especially those youth facing material precarity. My fieldwork draws from and investigates these debates in the current framing of masculinities in sports clubs, while highlighting the need for acknowledging a plurality of masculinities embodied in different sites encompassed within the realm of the club.

Chapter 4

"Ambition in the Desert": Training to Recognise Responsibilities

Introduction

Sports clubs encourage understanding and performing one's responsibilities as a prerequisite to valued masculinities. This argument will be displayed within different sites that make up the sports club. This chapter will begin by introducing different sites within the training field where I most frequently interacted with each club. The training sessions themselves represent spaces where each player is responsible to improve themselves as a machine for sporting success, activating better financial opportunities or improved status. Positional emphasis shows that responsibilities are not homogenous. Players see training as a test of dedication and a liminal space where access to status-changing games are negotiated. The chapter will then turn its attention to responsibilities toward community-building through a case study of repaired relationships after a fight. Team huddles and lift clubs show the importance of recognizing responsibilities within club hierarchies, and the ways in which these talks emphasize its importance to constructing masculinities. Not showing up for personal duty was the ultimate masculine failure. The chapter will then cover the ways sports organizations embed themselves in the histories of masculine identities at the club. It concludes by demonstrating how the club explicitly promotes ambition and providing for others as the marker of a useful man.

Construction Sites: Where is the Sports Club?

Sports clubs are structures made up of different social sites, all of which require each player to acknowledge and adhere to their responsibilities within that context in order to effectively embody and perform manhood. The theme of responsibility was unavoidable as I navigated through the field. Both sports clubs I worked with were made up of composite times and places. Some of these sites included the Upington City clubhouse; the DFC group chat[11]; team busses and carpools, training, social events throughout Upington, and management meetings, just to name a few. Training was where I interacted with each club most. Both teams trained on the premises of the local Technical and Vocational Education and Training (TVET) college. The field was expansive, bordered by a fence with a few gaps just wide enough to fit through. I sometimes entered this way, avoiding the long path around to the formal college entrance. Training happened every weekday at Upington City from 9.15 a.m. to 12.15 a.m., with players braving the sweltering sun. DFC would begin their training at 5.30 p.m., training on Mondays, Tuesdays and Thursdays. In the winter, these sessions would end when the field was encapsulated by debilitating darkness[12].

Even within the context of training, multiple social sites emerged, comprised of personnel, time, history and place. For example, when both teams

---

[11] A site which I did not have access to, except through player information.

[12] The TVET college field had no flood lights.

arrived at the training field, they ascended the bleachers, set their bags down and got changed. For the more professional Upington City, this meant an entire training kit which would alternate every other day. Both teams then engaged in warm-up drills. The football club had a full-time fitness coach/ physiotherapist to lead these sessions, while DFC players often negotiated their own personal warm-ups. After the warm-ups, the teams would gather in a circle while the coach addressed the goals for the proceeding session. At the end of the session, the circle would be formed again, and the head coach would frequently deliver passionate talks, often followed by the captain or assistant coaches. Each team had closing rituals, both engaging in prayer first. At each of these sites, club members had different roles to play.

Men as Mouldable Machines

While sites influenced the specific roles, each site was similar in promoting responsibilities that members were expected to know and adhere to. Analysis from key thinkers on masculinities in the South African context, corroborate this argument. According to Robert Morrell (2018:622):

> Boys and men do not have one mode of performing their masculinity. Different contexts have different arrangements of power which will require them to behave differently, to 'fit in'. Both context and choice are important and mutually related.

How then, do contexts and choices play into the club's shaping of masculine behaviours, conceptions and embodiment? The training field presents certain opportunities and conceptions, played out in/by the body. According to Mauss, the body shapes and is shaped by gendered traditions (Mauss, 1973). He (1973:78) argues that many men submit themselves to voluntary regimes of discipline to be moulded as an effective tool for sporting success. What is the club's position on training and its benefits for the masculine body? More importantly, how do players view training and their bodies? For Scarra, a senior player at Upington City who spent many years in the highest tier of South African football, the notion of selfless sacrifice towards the team goal of winning is how he understands what makes a good teammate and a good man – the broader iteration being sacrifice towards familial success.

His teammate Thabiso was significantly younger. When I asked him what a young man does in Upington during his free time, he told me how he goes to the park with his teammates and participates in a Christian homecell[13] group. He abstains from vices such as drugs and alcohol. "When I'm home [in Mamelodi], everything is loose. When I get on that bus [to Upington] to come play, I am going to work.". His sentiment reflects a theme from the Upington City players. Their body is their job. The trope of the disciplined, God-fearing and humble player was dominant in Upington City players' stories, and resonates with the conclusions made by Kovač in his research of young male footballers in Cameroon (Kovač, 2021:80). Financial activation rested on their ability to be fit enough to play, and to hone their skills through training. Player revelations on training – and the idea of voluntary discipline – seems to reflect a

[13] An informal, small church group, often comprised of youth. Homecells are especially prevalent in the Christian Revival Church (CRC), a popular Protestant denomination in South Africa.

view of their responsibility to sharpen the body as a weapon at the training grindstone, in order to effectively achieve sporting success.

Specialisation and Status

The shaping and training of the body is not homogenous, and the most effective masculine body looks different according to the roles the players take up. For example, in rugby, the forwards and the backs each have different jobs and often train separately at DFC. The sports club shapes the masculine body in different ways. For some, agility is valued above all else. For others, it is strength. In football, the goalkeepers stand out from the rest of the squad and undergo a different regime. At Upington City, they trained with their own specialised goalkeeping coach, an accommodating but strict man named Lawrence whose hefty physical presence was both reassuring and intimidating. The separation of training and emphasis on positional knowledge reflect the common thread of understanding responsibility, while showing that these responsibilities differ according to position at the club. Understanding and executing one's diverse and positional responsibilities is the common uniting thread which leads to unity and harmony in the club.

The training field also represented a liminal space, both for bodily shaping, and gaining status or access to status-changing games (Besnier and Brownell, 2012:445). Training is seen as a pathway to a starting berth for matchdays where not everyone can be accommodated.[14] Training allowed players to impress

[14] In football, only eleven players from either side are allowed on the field, while rugby teams are comprised of fifteen players.

the coaches with their skills and dedication. At DFC, some players were frustrated by management's affordance of game time to those deemed undeserved. I witnessed a conversation that demonstrated this frustration. On a bitterly cold night where the players had worked so hard it looked as though steam was rising from their heads, I was part of a lift club with three other members. Sindisa, a big forward who was at every practice I observed, made his feelings known about the team selection for the previous game. "These guys don't come to training but get to play", he grumbled. To him, training was a test of dedication, or rite of passage, allowing entry into the "real fun".[15] The field allowed members to win status and approval, both of the self and others.

To borrow from Clifford Geertz (1972:26) in his interpretation of Balinese cockfighting games, sporting status is a "story that [sporting men] tell themselves about themselves". Exceptional performances can lead to higher status, and even reverence. I felt this reverence as I witnessed a stunning goal from Upington City's star striker, Mali. His colleagues, coaches and a handful of spectators looked at each other in disbelieving confirmation after witnessing his volleyed goal into the top corner from around the halfway line. Everyone clapped. Sporting excellence, and the achieving sporting body is not the only encouraged aspect of training sessions.

---

[15] One of the main reason many players gave for joining DFC, was their alienation at United (a rival Rugby Club) where the selection policy was reportedly based on who the coach was friends with, or knew for longest. DFC is known for its meritocracy, where players are selected based on skill and performance.

Responsibility to Community

Community responsibility is a vital part of training. Training is fun. Mauss' idea of the body as a weapon is incomplete. In the sports club, the training man is also a body in contact with a community. Effort is acknowledged and there are constant shouts of encouragement to keep up the standards of the club. At DFC, the shouts, "*ons raak nie lazy nie*, boys!"[16] and "*urgency manne*"[17] commonly reverberated around the field. Amateur rugby clubs, especially amongst marginalized groups, are forms of community building (Morrell, 2018:621).

The narrative that the club serves as a purely competitive place where masculinities are negotiated in hierarchies is incomplete (Morrell, 2018). Bra Jack is a relatively new member at DFC. While many of the players have been there since the club's 2017 inception, he joined at the beginning of 2023. He comes from a footballing background, and often makes mistakes on the field, but he is accepted into the wider community, despite the occasional snigger at his misfortune. The sense of community is clearly prioritized in the story of Sindisa, who eventually became club captain. This is a second-hand account, detailed by one of the DFC members during an interview at a local coffee shop.

> Sindisa once tackled Marley hard in training. Marley said "*jou ma se poes*",[18] in reaction. Sindisa took it seriously. He *klapped*[19] Marley, very hard, and people

---

[16] "We don't get lazy, boys"

[17] "Urgency, men"

[18] An offensive Afrikaans verbal curse/insult. Directly translated to, "Your mother's cunt".

[19] smacked

had to break them up. It was awkward between them for a few weeks. They didn't greet or speak to one another. That was like one of the only times we had conflict like that. Anyways, after a while, Sindisa buys him a watch, and gathers the team together so he could apologize to Marley for his reaction.

While sporting success and physical domination is a factor, Sindisa prioritized the group dynamic, performing his role as a member that helps regulate a sense of togetherness in the team. This complements the framework of incompleteness and convivial relations with others as a staple of activation in Africa. The well-being of the structure was more important than his ego. According to Nyamnjoh (2017:260), "social visibility is facilitated by being interconnected with others in a communion of interests". Sindisa's morals and beliefs then influenced what is permissible and expected within the club, as evidenced by fewer violent incidents since, and his ascension in club leadership. The club creates an atmosphere of encouragement for those willing to do their duties, despite its difficulty. While Shaba, a defender at Upington City, freely admits to making mistakes, he says his coaches and teammates respect him because he gives his all and doesn't hide from his responsibilities. Maintaining community is a key responsibility for masculinities embedded in sports clubs.

The Huddle

The importance of accountability is reflected across the sites at DFC, despite role changes. The team huddle is a reflective space. After rigorous sessions, administrative issues and general club standards are addressed. I joined arm-in-arm with players, huffing and puffing from their exertion. The club hierarchy is felt more here than anywhere else. Coach Ash – founder and head coach – speaks first, sometimes followed by his assistants, or Sindisa as captain. This is not a free-for-all or forum, as evidenced by his strict silencing of those having private conversations in the circle.[20] There is still a fraternizing element and good jokes are welcome. Masculinities are regulated according to your role. For the listeners, you are expected to shut up. The speakers take different approaches, playing their role to galvanize team spirit or address concerns. Keppie, an assistant coach[21], enjoys discussing tactics while making parallel jokes and metaphors alluding to sexual deviance. Gibbs, a player/coach, takes the opportunity to encourage players or point out flaws, although the latter is rarely personally targeted.

Coach Ash meanwhile, often delivers passionate talks, akin to short sermons, often around the topics of behaviour, dedication, attitudes and being a good son, husband or father. The idea, often implicit, is that each individual take responsibility for how far away they are from the masculine ideal from the club, with certain dedicated players held up as examples to others. In this way, the club serves as a moralizing agent for Black masculinities, often linked to ideas akin to the "Protestant work ethic"[22] (Kovač, 2021:80). Team huddles close training – and match

---

[20] Public team meetings, where anyone is allowed to talk, do exist. These often manifest in crisis. However, everyone is allowed to talk and fraternize outside of the circle.

[21] Responsible for the backline training during sessions.

[22] Values such as discipline, hard work and humility are often linked to stoicism and a type of Protestant morality often preached by missionaries and espoused by young, working-class people (Kovač, 2021:90). The concept was popularized by Max Weber.

days – formally. At both clubs, it ends with prayer. The coach selects the divine intermediary as the players avoid eye contact. To my surprise, coach Ash called on me to pray upon my return to DFC observations in June. Status and meaning in club spaces are often activated by acceptance as a participant in ritual (Malaby, 2009). Being asked to pray helped ingratiate me into the team, a proverbial nod of acceptance from the man at the top of the club hierarchy. I had a role.

Load-Sharing

Lift clubs were the final aspect of training. A call for "*Vale, Vale, saam met my in die bakkie*"[23]rose up as players got rides home with their nearest car-owning teammate. Lift clubs presented drivers with the opportunity to help their teammates, especially in the dark, freezing cold June evenings. Race and class histories are inseparable from masculinities (Morrell, 2012; Ratele, 2016), and at DFC, and this influenced what players became responsible for. The following chapter will focus on intersectional analyses, although it is important to add here that almost all DFC's players were black and had working-class backgrounds. Most had no cars. Those that did were now expected to assist with transportation as long as it was reasonably close to their homes. This is a form of caring masculinities often overlooked when the focus is solely on power dynamics between men in hegemonic analyses (Elliott, 2016). I was a recipient of this form of care, where each driver would divide the responsibility of dropping players at their

[23] A call for all the players from Louisvale to hop into the member's pick-up truck in order to go home. Lousivale is a small Coloured suburb just outside of Upington.

convenience. When no-one else was available, I would get lifts with Coach Ash.

The common thread for "being a man" across the sites of the club was judged through the lens of how competently you lived up to your responsibilities. I witnessed an example of this when Coach Ash organized a team bus for an away game at Groblershoop, over 100 kilometres away from Upington. He asked all the players to join and contribute towards the bus costs. On the day, he was furious as some players organized individual transport with cars – without informing management of their plans. His disappointment was verbalized. The players had failed to live up to their responsibility and play the team game, rendering his efforts wasted. He paid the outstanding bus fare from his own pocket. The club was not neutral in influencing masculinities. Acceptance from the club aids the rite of passage into manhood (Keimbou, 2005). Failing your responsibility was indicative that there was need for personal growth, that there were persistent boyish elements in your manhood. Not showing up or taking responsibility was the ultimate masculine failure for most of my participants.

When is the Sports Club?

Histories are an integral part of determining contexts for different roles and responsibilities. Historical contingencies shape which aspects of identity and tradition are most heavily weighted in masculine performances within a particular social context (Besnier, et al., 2018:839)[24]. It's important not

[24] e.g., morality, politics, economic status, kinship, sexuality etc.

to consider Upington City or DFC in a vacuum. Sports like football, rugby and cricket, are integral parts of extra-curricular schooling activities besides the casual games that happen in communities (Morrell, 2018). When had sports clubs begun to influence its members' masculinities? Mali describes his first entry into football at grassroots level, where he "joined his older friends at eight years-old, playing Sunday league football in the area." Most players have been involved in organized team sports since adolescence.

Coach Ash speaks of his passion for working with young people. He coached and was heavily involved in organized rugby amongst schools in Upington. Many of his players have known him since their childhood. These histories influence personal responsibilities as well as identity perception in the group. Alexander, a player who grew up in Cape Town, speaks of his teammates intimate knowledge of each other and their roles in the game, simultaneously: "These guys have been playing together since school. The Flank[25] knows exactly what he must do. I'm still learning my position." A reflection perhaps of more than just tactical rugby, but the fluidity and negotiation of roles and niches within the structure. Sports clubs, therefore, have been important structures in constructing the masculinities of the young adults they comprise of since the days of their childhood.

[25] The numbers 6 and 7 in a rugby team, named after their position on the flanks of the scrum. They are typically the fastest of the forwards (big men).

Ambition, Provision and Personhood

There is significant investment in masculine development narratives outside of the sporting lens. Coach Nkosi at Upington City, calls himself a father to his players before his role as a coach. "The boys are people before they are players." Work done on the conceptions of manhood and youth masculinities in the African context, agree that navigating aspirations are inseparable from activation from boyhood to manhood in the ever-shifting world with its time-bound opportunities (Kovač, 2021; Meiu, 2017; Musariri, 2021; Fuh, 2012). For club members, the imminent threat of becoming a "useless man" by not showing long-term ambition (Kovač, 2021) was very real.

Ambition was one of Coach Ash's most rehashed sermons. Alexander told the story of an eye-opening encounter with Coach Ash. After a game on Saturday, he had gone clubbing. He stumbled through the streets on Sunday morning, drunk from the night's festivities, when Coach Ash drove by him on his family's way to church. "*Is jy befok in jou kop, Alex!? Hoe kan jy so lyk?*[26] I don't wanna see you like this again." This verbal barrage shook him. He also recognized that his coach was looking out for him. Coach Ash would later help organize his Curriculum Vitae and link him with his current job as a policeman, a breadwinner for his family. A large part of masculine identities in the sports clubs are linked to provision, whether through sporting activation or other work (Kovač, 2021:417). Shaba, like many other players, is focused on his ambitions because of his responsibilities at home, with a three-month old

[26] "Are you fucked in the head? How can you look like this?"

baby to feed. Ambition and aspirations were a common plea and motivational tool in Coach Ash's moralizing team huddles. Caring masculinities at the sports clubs operated in tandem with an ideal of the aspiring man, a man worth investing in, working towards something – raising the stakes of life through his ambitious action.

Conclusion

Throughout the club structure, and most evidently displayed in training sites, is the implicit motivation to understand and perform one's responsibilities. These responsibilities look different according to the individual's role. On the field, the masculine body is conceptualized as a weapon to be formed. This competitive warlike framing, however, is balanced by community responsibilities and the fun that training also produces. Meaningfully belonging to the sports club meant taking up your responsibilities, seen as the essence of masculinity in almost every site. Sport has reinforced this message for young boys since childhood in Upington and beyond. The club seems to explicitly promote ambition amongst in players, moralizing them into "useful men", never shirking their responsibilities – beyond the club.

Chapter 5

"*Ons As Bruin Manne*": Intersections of Race, Class, Sexuality and Ability

Introduction

Sports clubs shape and are shaped by the positionalities of its members which foster ideals of masculinities based on responses to particular social environments. This chapter will provide an intersectional analysis of embodied masculinities and promoted masculine ideals at play at DFC. At the time of my research, both DFC and Upington City's teams were exclusively male, and almost exclusively made up of Black men. This chapter begins by showing how racial backgrounds and cultural identities influence aspiration and ambition as encouraged ideals in response to the dangers of "useless masculinities" through vice, as opposed to narrow lenses framing them as victims or perpetrates. Sexuality, meanwhile, was a topic that was rarely spoken about seriously, and heterosocial masculinities were made visible and dominant at the club. It will then zoom in on ableism and class negotiation at the club where players with "unfit" bodies or middle-class status are often labelled as "soft", an effeminizing term for unappealing masculinities. Reproduction, sex and partying attitudes revealed complexities in embodied masculinities, with players operating as agents in determining the poles of permissible masculinities at the club. Intersectional analyses of masculinities reveal that masculinities are shifting, and which masculinities are preferred and made (in)visible through humour and public perception.

Ambitious Activation: Plight of the "Useless" Black Man

Ambition and responsibility are a response to social environments that often restrict Black masculinities due to simplified narratives or material constraints. Masculinities exist at intersections which influence what is permissible and encouraged as a response to the social environment (Oyewumi, 1997). Intersectionality is a key part of understanding masculinities (Mfecane, 2020; Ratele, 2016; Morrell, et., al., 2012) for young Black[27] men in Upington. Upington City was made up exclusively of Black men from various ethnic backgrounds. DFC, meanwhile, was mostly Black, with most members identifying as Coloured[28]. In three separate conversations with Coach Ash, he told me, "The problem with *our* boys/ *ons bruin manne*[29], is that they lack ambition. They don't want to do anything [meaningful] with their lives." He was referring to young Coloured men in Upington and the wider Northern Cape.[30] In

[27] I use Black under the Biko definition of Blackness in South Africa: those who have historically been marginalized on the basis of race, class and gender.

[28] Coloured is a cultural identity adopted by many South Africans. Despite its complex colonial past, I have employed it as a marker of significance and racialized reality that influences customs and behaviours.

[29] "us brown (Coloured) men"

[30] During one of his speeches in which he referred to "us Coloured men", he caught himself, acknowledging the presence of Wessels, a white man, in our presence. He quickly referred to Wessels as "Coloured by association", drawing laughter from the group.

Upington, much like in Buea, South-West Cameroon, the antidote to "uselessness" and submitting to the enslavement of drug and alcohol abuse in the community, is a life of hard work and focus towards a goal of success (Kovač, 2022:145). A kind of "Protestant Work ethic" underlies the moralizing mission of the sports club in response to poverty and purposelessness, a reality for many Black men in the region. Delinquency stories still dominate local media narratives about Black young men in Upington (e.g. IOL, 2021; EWN News, 2021; EWN News, 2021; thesouthafrican.com, 2022).

This book does not seek to undermine crime and violent masculinities. However, many young men negotiate an agency outside of the boundaries of perpetrators (of petty and domestic violence) or victims (of structural inequality or precarity or violence) (Fuh, 2012). Divine Fuh (2012:501) argues that young Black men look to impress their peers through status and prestige, driven – in the case of DFC and Upington City – by adhering to their responsibilities and focusing their actions on aspirations. The sports club, therefore, is a space of progression towards a masculine ideal and the negotiation of identity and agency in precarious situations e.g., youth unemployment[31]. It is a place for Black men to "just be free and not think about life[32]", but also a place to make their lives better through physical, social and financial activation. Aspirations and responsibilities are therefore crucial to how the

---

[31] Youth Unemployment in South Africa stands at a whopping 46,5% - as of May 2023 (Statistics South Africa). The large majority of this burden falls on Black and Coloured youth (statista.com)

[32] A quote from a DFC player on why he plays rugby.

sports club influences Black, and more specifically, Coloured masculinities in Upington.

Unserious Black Sexuality

Another aspect of intersectional masculinities is sexuality and ableism which, although separated in my writing, is part of racialised masculinities. It must be stressed that masculinities are embodied, negotiated, and enacted differently depending on different situations (Ammann and Staudacher, 2021:761). The following anecdotes are merely observations about intersections at which masculinities were played out. It does not seek to produce "completeness". Both clubs envision heterosexual masculinities in their ideals for being a "man". These conversations did not happen in the same way, however. On one occasion, I witnessed a player catcalling a woman who used the field as a thoroughfare. On another, an assistant coach compared preparing for a game to seeing an attractive girl on the side of the road and getting "warmed up for your wife back home". Coach Ash, meanwhile, described the responsibility and expectation of reliability in club participation to a happy, nuclear home. He encouraged the group to show up and be consistent in taking care of their wives and girlfriends as a tenet for being a good man – a responsible husband.

Black, sexual masculinities were often expressed through humour. Jokes alluding to homosexuality manifested themselves in a singular comment that was repeated at intermittent intervals during random sessions. One player would refer to the group as "*hol-naaiers*" (ass-fuckers) at the start of particular exercises. Sometimes the group would respond with laughter, while sometimes it was seemingly ignored. In the interviews I conducted, I would readily bring up class and race in my questions about the perception of masculine behaviours in the sports club. Sexuality was a subject, however, that I was unsure how to breach.

I would only acknowledge or explore sex, love or attraction in the rare conversations when the interlocutor brought it up. This carefulness stemmed from the atmosphere in Upington at large, and particularly my own knowledge of homophobia in sporting spaces where hetero-dominance is the order of the day. For many men in these settings, broaching sexuality was too close an inference to the possibility of queerness, a much maligned and othered sexual identity (Davis, 2017). To speak of homosexuality was by means of humorous microaggressions, and speaking seriously about sexuality could result in the closing of doors of access in my capacity as a researcher – not to mention personal stigmas in a town in which I spend significant chunks of my year. While I maintained a social standing identifying with dominant heterosocial norms, I lost any diligent or serious understanding of sexualities at the club, rendering "othered" identities hidden in this work. The sports club was not the place to discuss sexuality seriously.

A Soft Man: Class and Ableism

Class differences seemed to manifest more subtly. The general membership of the club seemed to be formerly disadvantaged South Africans, with families in the working classes, but in various stages of transitioning to middle-class lifestyles and symbols of wealth. A few players arrived in work uniforms, like mechanics and police officers, some only changing their footwear before jogging onto the field. Tien, an easy-going twenty-year old fullback for the club, revealed his understandings of class differences and its impact on the masculine performances at the club.

> "I always come to training with different cars, either mine or my father's or my brother's. The other guys see this and say 'Tien, he's rich, he's soft. He doesn't know what it means to struggle'." He continued as he slowly shook his head. "In the meantime, I'm also struggling. I also have to make sacrifices. That's part of life. You shouldn't compare. I'm just trying to be myself."

Men who were injured or unavailable were also brandished, albeit not in serious tones, with the brush of softness. "*Die is n sagte man*"[33], was the jeer of a handful of players towards the entrance of one of the players who had missed half the session due to discomfort, and was not committing himself to tackles. Ableism on the field rendered those who were unable to use their bodies ideally as "soft", an effeminate quality.

Many times, I felt self-conscious for not playing, and my middle-class status. I did not want the label of "soft", an unappealing feminization in the space. Early on, I positioned myself as a writer and not a player – an honest position – which allowed me to escape the tag of soft. I navigated my roles and responsibilities dutifully. Not getting tackled was a bonus. I, too, was entangled in intersections and the negotiation of my own masculinities and approval of status amongst club members (Fuh, 2012). A big part of sporting masculinities is based on replication of

---

[33] "This is a soft man".

other men, or the sharpening of the body as a machine (Mauss, 1973). If the masculine body is rendered unfit, a dull, useless weapon (to draw from earlier imagery), it detracts from activation as a hardworking, heterosexual Black man in the space, an indication of the reproduction of ableist sporting influences on masculine identities.

Being Fruitful: Pleasure, Partying and Personal Choices

Reproductivity and sex was another aspect of enquiry that fluttered around masculine identities, often without being discussed explicitly. I did notice, however, a divergence from Uroš Kovač's (2021:80) trope of the two masculine extremes within sports clubs: the monogamous, disciplined and humble player as a direct antonym of the lazy, flashy and sexually promiscuous type of player. While there were players who seemed to lean towards either side – a quality of a trope – the club structure did not seem to disapprove of sexual promiscuity, or partying within limits. After a big win in Groblershoop, the DFC bus was fairly silent for ten minutes. This was not good enough. We were not at a funeral, were we? The players took initiative, booming Brenda Fassie's "Weekend Special" through the sound system. We sang heartily. This was a winning mood!

Some of the players were pressing me to talk to Hendrik, the big forward sitting next to me – whose wide frame took up half of my seat too. They wanted to know what I thought about his fathering of eight children by the age of thirty-two, a fact that some mocked while others spoke about in awe. Hendrik was eager to talk. He reminisced on the days of his younger youth, and his extravagant excursions throughout South Africa. He urged me to enjoy life while I'm young – an enjoyment based on pleasure-seeking in multiple forms.

Meanwhile, one of the players who had told me earlier in the week about his intense discipline and feats of fitness, was the life of the post-game party. In a similar twist of the expected narrative, a player named Ronaldo, who had been dubbed the team's pastor, due to his zealous religious beliefs and non-promiscuity, had earlier exchanged innocuous threats to fight a dissenting teammate. The complexity of masculinities, influenced by race, class, and other intersections – revealed an in-betweeness of the poles of the tropes of sporting masculinities. Reproduction, promiscuity and their relation to the good life, seemed to be mostly at the whim of the individual and their histories and social environments, and not a major property of senior club influence. This indicated player and intra-personal influences on the sports club, meaning that its influence shifts according to member temperament and positionality.

Conclusion

Intersectional analyses of masculinities at the clubs revealed a complex deviation from popular narratives from both media and literature. The intersections at which masculinities operate cannot be separated from its performances. They revealed new ideals, based on racial histories, sexuality, class dynamics, reproduction, ableism and indulgence. Coloured young men in the area are often framed as shifting between the status of perpetrator and victims of structural violence. The sports club promotes activation beyond these narrow poles. Sexuality, within the club confines, was addressed through humour and not particularly seriously – apart from heterosexual ideals. Class dynamics and the body were intrinsically linked to ideals of the "hard" man, with "soft" masculinities frowned upon by the players[34]. Finally, reproduction and different understandings of partying and the good life, show that players navigate difficulties and encouragement between the tropes of "disciplined" and "reckless" men, showing how masculinities are more and less complicated than had been theorized. The influence of the sports clubs on these masculinities are shifting and respond differently at various intersections of masculinities, and are regulated in part, by the players own conceptions and intersectional identities.

---

[34] In the next chapter, we will delve into a response to the promotion of "the hard man" in the face of crisis.

Chapter 6

"Saying Hello and Saying Goodbye": Recognition, Motivation and Appropriate Masculine Intimacy

Introduction

Acknowledgement rituals carry great importance in validating other men and determining permissible forms of masculine care DFC. They re-establish existing positions in club hierarchies and allow members to award prestige to other men in the club. These rituals simultaneously symbolize possibility and openness to dialogue and mobility in club status. Handshakes, especially after games, re-introduce appropriate heterosocial distance, and shape public care and intimacy between players. This chapter will examine these claims by drawing on literature theorizing hierarchy and the shifting nature of prestige in sports clubs. It will then analyse the handshake in companion with literature evaluating what care is allowed in sporting masculinities. During the research period, risk, danger and care responses emerged as an unexpected theme after the death of two players as a result of injuries sustained on the rugby field. This opened questions about player motivations to play rugby in the face of danger. Freedom and joy through play was a common thread in player responses. The mourning period in the aftermath of the events shows that while sports clubs show care for players in a myriad of ways, emotional sensitivity is often left out of conceptions of appropriate masculine being within club structures.

The club did, however, take steps to provide more tangible care in future through a new emergency medical fund. Through the tragedies, I will argue for incompleteness in conceptions of what motivates sporting masculinities, and how appropriate care is determined in club spaces through player perspectives on mourning and sensitivity.

Saying Hello in Handshakes: Acknowledgement Rituals in the Field

It took me several weeks to explicitly notice the ever-presence and frequency of acknowledgement rituals at the club. When I first got to DFC training, I did not know anyone. I greeted the players verbally. When Coach Ash arrived, he called me over and he extended his hand to me. I had spoken to him before via WhatsApp but I did not know his face. I remember being embarrassed that he had had to call me over, especially because he was my elder.[35] As the players got to know me, they would come over to take my hand, a sign that I was being recognized by the group. This would often be accompanied by a, *"Wat sê die man?*[36] ", or *"Awê Sam/bru/masekind*[37] ". This always happened at the start of practice. Handshakes at the end of practice were also commonplace. Despite the almost constant greeting that occurred each time a player entered the field of training, I first became explicitly aware of the importance of the handshake at the game I attended

[35] In my family on both parent's sides, it was expected that younger people initiated greeting with their elders.

[36] What do you have to say man? – A casual greeting akin to 'how are you?'

[37] Variations on a colloquial form of, "Hi bro".

against another amateur team, the Groblershoop Eagles.

That morning, members shook hands the first time as the team met at a local field to finalize trip details. After getting onto the bus, we arrived in Groblershoop where the players began warm-up drills. Before the game began, each player clasped hands again, often accompanied by a hefty tap on the shoulder – a pre-match ritual to wish each other good luck. A sense of solidarity seemed to be instilled. After the game players shook hands again, this time extending the ritual to the opposing team. When each player departed the bus, the final round of greetings commenced. This does not include the occasional handshakes exchanged between a substituted player and his coach and teammates. Female spectators, meanwhile, were generally greeted with hugs or waves, as opposed to the plethora of variations of handshakes between the club's men. What is the value of a ritual that can occur up to five times with the same person in one day? Why would anyone need to greet that much?

Theorising Greeting and Handshakes

For the DFC members I spoke to, acknowledgement was never an explicitly important component of masculine constructions through the club's social sites. In fact, when observing the sheer quantities of greeting, I doubted my own observations of its anthropological value. I had been a member of sports clubs for years. In the mornings at school, I would join a circle of boys - often with a football being juggled between them – and would go around to greet each person by hand, a ritual not specific to any particular group of boys, but seemingly exclusive to hetero-normative appearing boys. Girls and feminine individuals wouldn't receive the specialized daps reserved for the fraternity. We never spoke about it. Why would we need to speak about something that *just happened* every morning? The ordinary nature of greeting, especially in tightly bounded communities, seems to give it the appearance of arbitrariness (Morgan, 2015:128). Sheryl Hamilton (2017:55), in her work *Rituals of Intimate Legal Touch,* argues that while greetings are normative, they are not arbitrary. It is an imperative part of wider peaceful interaction, and the handshake specifically is a symbol of people united towards some form of common co-existence or goal (Hamilton, 2017:55).

It is important here to distinguish between greeting as a social practice, and handshakes as a phenomenon. In this book, greetings often include, but are not limited to, handshakes. Handshakes, meanwhile, often denote greeting rituals, and are always embedded in ritual ceremony (Hamilton, 2017:56).

I will be analysing masculine rituals of acknowledgement at DFC in a twofold manner. The first uses the lens of greeting as the meeting place between existing hierarchies of power and acknowledgement, and a place of potential for new possibilities of sociality (Morgan, 2015:125). The second will look at the handshake in defining permissible social intimacy (Hamilton, 2017:64), and its meaning as a form of appropriate masculine care at DFC and beyond.

As discussed in chapter 4, a fight broke out between two players at DFC whom I called Sindisa and Marley. Their conflict emerges within the bounds of the first analytic lens. Popular literature on greeting theorizes it as an “access ceremony”, (Goffman, 1971:74) although the question of what is being made accessible appears to be shifting according to context, and difficult to measure. Hamilton (2017:55) believes that in less porous communities with initiated members like sports clubs, it is access to recognition and social inclusion. The interlocutor who told me the story made it a point of including that both didn’t greet the other for weeks after the incident. Not greeting is significant, despite the fact that both attended training and played together without fighting again. Greeting is performative. It is an example of how young men in sports clubs attribute and receive prestige and recognition to and from each other (Fuh, 2012). To quote Fuh (2012:504): “young men [affirm] identities, repair fissures, and compete for attention and visibility through a myriad of performative displays”. The fissures between Sindisa and Marley were evidenced most clearly by their opting out of the acknowledgement ritual so embedded in DFC practices. Neither were ready to offer recognition of the other’s place in the social order, or prestige economy of DFC.

Pyramids with Elevators: Affirmation and Possibility through Touch

Player interactions with myself and Coach Ash highlighted how the form of acknowledgement reinforces status and produce possibilities for growth beyond one’s current status in the club. Each player made it a point to physically acknowledge their teammates as they arrived at training or matchdays. As I began to know the names and have conversations with more DFC members, more would come and take my hand despite my lack of involvement in the explicit training objective – playing rugby. This pleased me. Fuh (2012:504) argues that social recognition rituals in prestige economies is the endorsement of potential, identity and belonging as an agent within the group dynamic – a fitting representation of what I felt was happening, albeit without such eloquent articulation. Handshakes seemed a particularly powerful tactile symbol of possibility – the acknowledgment that both parties have deemed each other acceptable to touch, and a gateway to further conversation (Morgan, 2015; Hamilton, 2017).

Concurrently, observing player interactions with Coach Ash revealed the ways in which authority is reinforced in acknowledgement rituals. Coach Ash almost always received a formal handshake. The nature of the handshake denoted a relationship different to that of the informally acknowledged teammates. In addition, it was the players' prerogative to go to the coach and shake his hand. On countless occasions, our conversations at the base of the metal bleachers were politely interrupted by arriving players. Each would acknowledge coach with a formal handshake accompanied by the word "coach(ah[38])", offering me a more informal handshake, before continuing on to the rest of the group. According to Hamilton (2017:57):

> the meaning and work of a handshake depends upon the manner of presentation of self of the respective parties, the understanding of each by the other, and the interplay of its multiple layers of context. Its import and effect must always be assessed in interaction with the range of gestures, modes of touching, and speech acts with which it is entwined.

---

[38] A colloquial variation on coach.

Through differences in handshake styles and verbal acknowledgement, players reinforced the respectful distance between themselves and Coach Ash, gaining access to certain benefits through his recognition. In this way, unspoken hierarchies and new masculine possibilities emerged through modes and variations of acknowledgement rituals at DFC.

Masculine Care, Touch and Heteronormative Boundaries

I remained confounded on one element of the gameday experience. The DFC players showed camaraderie and zealous willingness to acknowledge the opposing team after the game. The players shook hands with the opposition, before interlocking arms with them in a big circle for post-match speeches, thanks and prayers. Then everyone got together and smiled for a group photograph. I had just witnessed eighty minutes of men aggressively battering into each other in attempt to win back the leather oval. One had been carried off in a stretcher. Why were they so happy to shake the hands of those who had been their bitter enemies minutes prior?

A combination of literature on appropriate touch and care, and Coach Ash's philosophies helped provide an angle of explanation for this phenomenon. In answering why the post-game handshakes persist in the light of pandemic culture[39], Hamilton (2017:64) argues that it holds importance

---

[39] Theorised as the collective affective experience of living with the constant awareness of germ spread and pandemics (Hamilton and Gerlach, 2014), especially prevalent in 2023 – South African societies living in the wake of the Covid-19 pandemic.

for re-ordering appropriate distance and forms of caring public touch in heterosocial masculine spaces. While contact sport temporarily suspended such distance and care, the handshakes re-establish it (Hamilton, 2017). Coach Ash revealed that the tendency to greet and shake hands was not present at all games.

> Too many of the boys take it personally. Then rugby is not for you. You got beat in the game, *nou wil jy klap en steek*[40]. I've always believed, you go to battle and when it's done, you shake hands, say "well-played", and have a beer with your brother from the other team.

Two analogies stood out from this quote. The analogy of battle alludes to the physical struggle of the rugby game, but also its bounded nature. The field is the battleground for eighty minutes, and afterwards, you are "brothers" together in the wider world – an allusion to the fraternizing aspect of sporting masculinities. The rugby game has ended, and a new game of sociality emerges with its own iterations of strategy and combinations of competence and improvisation for success (Bourdieu, 1990:67). Coach Ash highlights the handshake and shared beer as an implicit strategy for success in the new game, relationship-building. Drawing from Pierre Bourdieu's (1990) *The Logic of Practice*, post-game handshakes serve as a symbol that the rugby field has been suspended and the social field now hosts a new game.

Part of the convivial socialising expected of sporting masculinities is based on a shared understanding and respect of the tough, competitive nature of the prior game. Robert Morrell (2017:630)

---

[40] "Now you want to hit and stab [your opponent]."

believes that the prestige in contact rugby partly stems from the "fierceness of the battle, which is likened to combat, because of the danger, risk", and the "recognition of being better than your opponents". The recognition rituals in the aftermath of the game are therefore a part of reinforcing the prestige of rugby for sporting masculinities, signalling the end of the battle, and re-introducing appropriate structures of care, touch and public intimacy in a new social game – especially in the aftermath of a joint rugby game rife with risk and danger.

Saying Goodbye

Risk, danger and mourning emerged as an unexpected theme during my DFC observation period. I received a lift home with Coach Ash after my first practice back in June. He revealed to me that in the space between my February observations and June, two players had tragically died as a result of injuries they sustained on the field of play. After the second tragedy, the season had been postponed, and practices were halted. Preparations were just now being made for the return of amateur rugby. DFC was not in a good place. Most were still grieving. Some players had informed club management that they would not return for the season. They were re-evaluating their own lives and the importance of rugby in the wake of such devastating disasters – for some, the loss of a lifelong friend.

The coach expressed his frustration that many of the members were not willing to be vulnerable and talk about their fear or the fact that they were still grieving. For him, this repression manifested in emotional dishonesty. He believed some would rather make excuses and not show up, than speak about what was on their minds. A week later, I asked Alexander and Tien about the aftermath of the bereavement. Alex believed most of his teammates were shaken by the news. For them, it was a wake-up call about the sport's dangers, and they sympathised with their teammates who had left.

> All of us know the possibility [of death] is there, but you don't think of it because it hardly ever happens. Their deaths made it real. A lot of guys had to think, how important is rugby really?

Tien corroborated this viewpoint. In addition to devastating the deceased players' closest friends, many feared it was going to happen to them the next time they jogged out to play. He sympathised, but had decided to keep playing. What motivated the remaining young men to keep playing in the face of death and mourning? And how did the sports club structure facilitate permissible masculine forms of mourning and grief within its social zones? I return to the players and their experiences in an attempt to find answers.

Why keep Playing?

The players enjoy rugby! Much of the literature on masculine motivations to participate in a social zone which presents death as a real possibility, is predicated on hegemonic masculine interpretations of the "warrior" and the "tough guy" image. Some theorists believe that the status rewards for men outweigh the fear of serious injury through physical sports (Robinson, 2004:120). Robert Morrell (2017:630) asserts that part of the reason that status is increased in organized club rugby participation is the danger and risk of serious injury, itself. The danger increases player enjoyment because the intensity and stakes are higher. The responses I received from DFC players, however, point to different motivations that seem to argue for less complexity.

The common answer to questions of persistence and motivation was that the players still really enjoyed rugby and the community at DFC. "When it's my time (to die), it's my time. I'm not gonna let that stop me from doing what I love."[41] Many spoke about the freedom they felt from the problems they faced off the field. This attitude is best encapsulated by the words of Bernard Magubane, who at the height of Apartheid oppression, said of the influence of club sport on player joy:

> Momentarily their emotional life which is often subdued and repressed during the week...is allowed to break through.... The drudgery which their life imposes on them is temporarily forgotten.

For many players, this freedom through masculine play was ample motivation to maintain club activity in the face of tragedy.

(In)Appropriate Care

While DFC encouraged certain forms of care and fostered a spirit of unity, it was not a place where players felt open to express their more vulnerable emotions like sadness and grief. Coach Ash believed the guys were too macho to share their feelings. But if he was at the pinnacle of the club hierarchy and clearly wanted his players to open up, why hadn't it

[41] A quote from Alex.

happened? I asked Alex about the club's forums for venting. His response was matter-of-fact.

> "The coaches did speak about it, yes. There were meetings where we could speak our mind… but I'm not there to talk about my stuff from home. The guys are there to practice, not to listen to my shit."

I interpreted Alex's "stuff from home", to be those feelings that spoke to his vulnerability. Tien, meanwhile, believed that while the mourning period was sobering, it had not changed him. He believed that life was rife with tragedies that one must "go through, deal with, and mourn. But after that, you just have to carry on with your life." Coach Ash's frustration with player failure to vocalize sensitive emotion is perhaps a reflection of Ratele's (2022:32) belief that "most men learn to cordon off their vulnerability", making the sports club an inappropriate place to express such feeling.

Incompleteness is present as a recurring theme in this analysis on masculinities, and problematic dichotomies between DFC members as players and people (or "hard" men and "soft" men) are blurred through alternate displays of care and expression at the club, demonstrating the messiness of life and its interconnections (Nyamnjoh, 2017:255). Despite players not believing in DFC's social spaces as the proper forum to be vulnerable in, the tangible battle with death and loss created other forms of motivation, solidarity and appropriate forms of care.

I remember standing arm-in-arm with players as Sindisa discussed how important it was to show up and be dedicated to the team cause. "These guys next to you must trust you. You're putting your life on the line for your brothers!" In this way, the tragedies were a source of galvanization of team spirit, while revealing the club structure's limitations on what is deemed appropriate masculine emotion in its zones of sociality. Sports clubs tend to teach co-operation, care and love for other men in a plethora of manners, but rarely foster emotional honesty or human sensitivity (Kidd, 2013:559). Emotional sensitivity is not commonplace in the DFC structure.

People first, Players second

Through the emerging theme of death and risk, the club also showed its care towards players and the value of the man and masculine body beyond its usefulness to rugby. One of the ways this was shown was the forum created in the wake of the tragedies, where open meetings were held to discuss ways forward for the club, and the mood of the members. In these meetings, unlike in team huddles, anyone could volunteer their opinion.

The deaths and their impacts were discussed frankly, and in the aftermath, there was no evidence of the romanticizing of death in rugby, a shift from the claim of the warrior man as a model for hegemonic masculinity (Morrell, 2017:630). At this meeting, tangible care was discussed. Both players, according to the reports I had heard[42], had been severely weakened by the lack of effective care from their local public hospitals. More effective care was expensive, and neither had had access to medical aid. The club began an emergency medical fund off the basis of this meeting. The fund's purpose was the

[42] It must be stressed that my work and perspectives are consistently incomplete. Here I have gathered general opinions around the club, a valuable contribution of incompleteness to bring to an incomplete table of understanding.

provision of excellent medical care in the event of another traumatic injury. For the players I spoke to, this was a form of assurance that the club did not see the masculine body as disposable, or Mauss' (1973) machines, but that it actually cared about player wellbeing. A touching tribute on the club's Facebook page remains as a legacy to the departed players. May they rest in peace.

Conclusion

Acknowledgement rituals such as greeting and handshakes, reveal the existing order and prestige located within club hierarches and recognition as a man. Simultaneously, however, it reveals the possibilities for conversation and friendship as an agent in the not-so-rigid club structure. Both handshakes, and player responses to the fatal tragedies that occurred on the field, reveal the club's influence on what is deemed permissible forms of masculine expressions of care, touch, emotional honesty and public intimacy. The aftermath of the player deaths also reveals the joy and freedom that players feel when playing rugby, beyond the status or prestige associated with motivations to play and be involved in sports clubs. The provision of an emergency medical fund via an open meeting forum shows how DFC cares for its players beyond just their contributions as a rugby-playing body.

Chapter 7

The Comrade, the Cross and the Crucible: Effective Tools for Affective Health

Introduction

Sports clubs give young men in Upington more opportunities to fraternize and address mental health concerns through structures which encourage interconnectivity. The affective health of young men are often ignored in the shadows of totalizing popular narratives, such as *toxic masculinity*. Another reason for the perceived silence on the matter is the private ways in which many black, heterosexual men express affective struggle. During the interview process, men's mental health was a common topic of conversation almost solely driven from player perspectives. A combination of religious togetherness, kinship and gendered mentorship were cited as key to maintaining healthy mental wellbeing and activating a more stable sense of self. While these tools and modes of expression were often situated in different parts of the sports club and with different groups, they drew on social bonds introduced to and by players in club spaces. While the stories of mental health concerns and successes share similar themes with many of the players I interviewed, they are not completely homogenous, nor should they be.

This chapter will look at men's mental health as an emerging, but often-ignored contemporary talking point before drawing on literature which reflects a turn in forms of expression through agency against rigid ideas of gender and social media. It will then break down each of the three most common coping and support mechanisms: religion, friendship and mentorship in player experiences and how they are reinforced through club-enforced habits, events and rituals. It will argue for interconnectivity as a tool for men to express themselves, facilitated by the club as a social frontier. Finally, the chapter will conclude by arguing for the acknowledgement of incompleteness present both in narratives about men through mental health awareness, and in the dominant positive narrative regarding the club's effect on mental health presented in this ethnography. A single story about *the* influence of sports clubs on men's mental health experiences should be avoided.

An Underestimated Struggle

During my interviews and interactions with club members, I hadn't intended on drawing on mental health as a major talking point about masculinities in the sports club. I was more focused on player understandings of what it meant to be a man. I also wanted to avoid leading questions that would frame the participants as victims or benefactors of social injustice. My first formal interview was conducted with Shabba, a senior defender at Upington City FC. As the conversation increased in depth, I asked him about his calm reaction to Coach Nkosi, who had singled him out for a verbal barrage earlier that morning. He revealed his struggles with anger in the past and how he overcame it during his time in Upington. During his story, which will be told later in this chapter, he reflected, "For us, it's very difficult to speak about our mental problems. Men's mental health isn't [seen as] important." My very next interview featured one of the younger players who spoke about mental health out of his own, and in a similar vein. He described mental health as an "underestimated" part of being a man. The following day, the two interviewees I spoke with mentioned aspects of mental health such as anxiety, depression, and fluctuating thoughts about self-worth. They claimed that these struggles and experiences were an intrinsic part of their growth as interdependent men. They learned who they could rely on. Mental health became one of the key conversations introduced by the players.

Is Mental Health in the Mind?

Interconnectivity emerged as a common theme in the problems associated with mental health. It is difficult to provide a fixed definition of mental health. There is a noticeable lack of uniformity in finding the boundaries or limits of mental health because of its frequent correlation to wider economic and structural problems, or familial disputes and disputes with others and self (Reihling, 2022). For this reason, the phrase *Affective health* is utilized by Anthropologist Hans Reihling (2022:1) to describe "a dynamic between human struggles for interconnectivity and autonomy". In popular conversation, masculinities and conversations around men's mental health have often been foregrounded by medical models which prioritise the individual and pathology (Reihling, 2022). This chapter is not an attempt to diagnose the mental conditions of players or argue for one particular view about men's mental health. Anthropologist David Bukusi (2020:2) argues that overemphasis on medical terminology does not do justice to the experiences of many African men, whose affective struggles are expressed through their interactions with others, and not in specialized health facilities.[43]

> We have observed that for [African][44] men, their daily struggles to reduce troublesome and confusing thoughts often do not bring them to the clinic, but rather to other kinds of gendered spaces of work and leisure that provide a valued sense of forward momentum amidst the constant, looming threat of stagnation and boredom, thereby mitigating particular problems of time (Bukusi, Fast and Myoer, 2020:2).

The sports club is an important "gendered space of work and leisure". The players of Upington City FC spend six out of seven days in their week training and living in the clubhouse, while DFC players often

---

[43] Francis Nyamnjoh (2023) makes the argument that exclusivity in healthcare policies that prioritise modern medicine have left majority populations both alienated and inadequately cared for in the postcolonial state. This argument is epistemologically backed by authors like Hugo ka Canham (2023) who demonstrate the inadequacy of historically accepted psychological terminology like Freud's "melancholia" in diagnosing the affective health of people in rural Mpondoland. For a more in-depth conversation on appropriate health measures and inclusive approaches which foreground mainstream-silenced indigenous approaches, see the above works. This section takes an Anthropological and more conversational approach to the subject in the lives of the participants from Upington.

[44] Their study was conducted in various sites in East Africa, although its applicability is startling amongst previously disadvantaged groups in the wake of colonialism and Apartheid. This does not necessarily exclude white Africans from the conversation, but highlights the lack of efficacy of the clinic amongst black men throughout historically-contingent imaginings of the continent.

train until the sun has disappeared, while balancing full-time jobs and families.

This chapter will argue for the acknowledgement of club and wider community structures, such as religion, friendship and mentorship as a major positive factor in many players' experiences of mental health issues. All of the issues - which all interviewees consented to have shared in this ethnography - are concerned with struggles in the realms of interconnectivity and autonomy. This chapter will use the terms *Affective health* and mental health interchangeably. This is an attempt at mirroring the language used by players and the wider public regarding Affective masculinities and men's struggles. Hopefully the anecdotes from the players, spark important conversations about vulnerability and affective health within sporting communities that are often overlooked in conversations about men's mental health. This is both a call for academia to renew vigour in research around masculinities and for men to challenge stigma around speaking up and attending to affect as an ethical imperative.

Isolation and Incomplete Pathology

Popular discourses and performances reifying masculinities as a singular phenomenon often overlook, and help foster, the isolation and invulnerability that accompanies affective suffering, or mental unwellness. Masculinities have often been associated with various tropes of behaviour and habits that gender men in relation to groups that have been marginalized by capitalist, colonial and patriarchal systems of power (Newman, et.al., 2022:855). The phrase *toxic masculinity* has become a popular term for describing unhealthy or violent stereotypically masculine behaviours (Boulton, 2023). This phrase typically draws on widespread moral tropes on the type of man one should generally avoid becoming. *Toxic masculinity* has drawn many into important public discussions about gender and its impact on behaviour (Boulton, 2023). The phrase, however, remains problematic as it presents an essentialised and ahistorical view on masculine performances, removing the agency from the men caught up in its shady umbrella (Waling, 2019). Anthropologist Jack Boulton, who investigated the phrase in public debates in Namibia - its border just over an hour away from Upington by car - describes the limits of the term. "Toxic masculinity becomes tautological: men and masculinities are toxic because they are toxic, and nothing more" (2023:230). The singular use of masculinity also leaves little room for incompleteness, while its adjective reinforces a static diagnosis of this singular masculinity.

One of the reasons that men's mental health is overlooked when addressing *toxic masculinity*, is the invulnerable performance of manhood present within the trope (Reihling, 2022:149). Some men, enchanted by the possibilities of power in patriarchal social systems, seek to *live up* to the tropes of being toxic, refusing to engage with others to address affective struggle outside of violence and destructive behaviours. However, these performances hurt these men as well as those closest to them (Boulton, 2023). In South Africa, discourse about mental illness is gendered and racialized. According to Reihling (2022), black heterosexual men are less likely to admit to mental health issues because of the fear of being pathologised or institutionalised, or forfeiting their strength or attractiveness to others through an admittance of weakness. While physical and sexual violence is commonly associated with toxic masculinities, one defining, yet often-ignored feature, are antisocial behaviours and the dismissal of treatment or even conversations about mental health - sometimes leading to self-harm and involuntary social isolation (Newman, et.al., 2022:856).

Both in popular narratives about men and masculinities, and in medical models of individual mental health, the importance of interconnectivity with others to address problematic behaviour are overlooked. In these singular stories which can claim legitimacy in the absence of important Anthropological work, men that shy away from social connection as a response to affective struggles are ignored or uncritically viewed as "traditional", or "toxic" (Ratele, 2013). I do not intend to ignore the alarming rates of femicide and Gender-Based Violence that continue to plague women in Southern Africa (Gqola, 2007; Mohamed, 2023). The perpetrators of these atrocities are predominantly men (Musariri, 2021:889). I am, however, presenting the dominant discourses around masculinities and showing how these narratives often overlook affective masculinities, and the multiplicity of ways in which men are encouraged or expected to express their affective struggles (hooks, 2004). Indeed, toxic, or traditional masculinities, are part of an incomplete, yet expanding vocabulary in theorising gender. Incompleteness provides the Anthropologist with a framework to consider nuance and the shifting dynamics of gender, best attending to the changing affects of men's mental health. Incompleteness also argues for interconnectivity and the importance of relying on others to practice identity and conviviality (Nyamnjoh, 2017). Interconnectivity enables social visibility (Nyamnjoh, 2017:260-261). Popular narratives about men and medical models of mental health can render the affective health of young Black men, and indeed these men themselves, invisible and inaudible. These narratives are incomplete, and do not do justice to the hopeful possibilities and alternative forms of masculinities emergent within the sports club, and wider society. Many young men feel free to avoid playing into the trope of toxic masculinity. Social isolation, in these cases, gives way to interconnectivity as "appropriate" forms of masculine affective expression.

Becoming the "New" South African Man

While "traditional" masculinities are still at play in South Africa[45], young men have agency in negotiating conversations about mental health beyond tropes of traditional masculinities and toxicity. A relatively recent Psychological study asked a racially mixed group of young South African men about their opinions on men's mental health struggles (Bantjes, Kagee and Meissner, 2017). The participants attributed South Africa's alarming rate of male suicides to feelings of social disconnectedness, not belonging and the pressures - and shame of not living up to certain masculine ideals and expectations (Bantjes, Kagee and Meissner, 2017:233) Awareness of gender construction has become more mainstream in South Africa (Mfecane, 2018:298). Conversations about mental health, previously dominated by white men in Apartheid South Africa, have also become a less stigmatized venture. The young men in the study

---

[45] Kopano Ratele (2013) makes an important critique of the unreflective ideas that accompany the moniker of traditional masculinities, questioning the notion of masculinities that exist outside of tradition.

attributed improvements in their own mental health to exposure to information and debate on social media platforms. They also believed that their generation was experiencing the relaxation of certain, previously non-negotiable masculine norms (Bantjes, Kagee and Meissner, 2017). This has been true for the employment and performance of my own masculinities.

This is not to say that I am free from the bounds of gendered restriction. Gendered experiences and performances still influence permissible behaviours (Oyewumi, 1997). Young adults are still embedded in systems in which they negotiate permission to act outside of gendered expectations (Moore, 2022:183). The pressure to adhere to hegemonic performances of "macho", strong black masculinities still linger around my experiences, and sometimes dictates who I feel comfortable letting my guard down with. I have witnessed family members attribute the depression of a young male cousin to weakness and a poor religious foundation. There is, however, a greater freedom to converse with my peers – and even the aforementioned family members – about my emotional well-being than I felt in my high school years. The young men in the study hold similar views about the freedoms to discuss mental health for men in recent years. They claimed that social media, and heightened knowledge around the social constructions and flexibility of gendered performance, have allowed them to feel more liberated in sharing mental health concerns (Bantjes, Kagee and Meissner, 2017). This increased agency in discussing mental health outside of "traditional", dismissive macho tropes was present in conversations at the sports club.

Non-Scalibility: Mapping Dynamic Structures

The sports club reinforces and challenges traditional masculinities as it reflects wider societal shifts. In an article about the value of maintaining orthodox masculinities for sports club stakeholders, American sociologist Eric Anderson (2009) argues that because of dominant boyhood cultures, participation in competitive team sports have been made almost non-negotiable for men whose constructions of masculinities rely on sporting fraternity and a "hypermasculine" body ready to be sculpted. Testimony from experienced players like Mali and Scarra from Upington City, and even the younger Alexander and Tien from the Defence Force Collegiates (DFC), show how sports have been an intrinsic part of their masculine development and expression since they were kids. Most had been involved in team sports since before they could remember. Anderson goes on to say:

> Competitive teamsports therefore exist as a microcosm of society's gendered values, myths and prejudices about gender, but they also actively construct boys and men to exhibit, value and reproduce traditional notions of masculinity—stratifying them in accordance with a hegemonic form of masculine dominance (2009:4).

What Anderson fails to account for is the incompleteness and possibilities present even in seemingly socially accepted modes of representation. While DFC and Upington City teem with competing societal views of gender and ideal masculine behaviours – they are after all, products of, and located in broader societal attitudes - the microcosm is not a complete one.

Within these clubs, many of their young men have attempted to distance themselves from the values and socially debatable views of the "traditional man". I do not want to fall into post-apartheid public literature trends simultaneously co-opted and critiqued in Masculinities studies in South Africa. These trends presents a "positive masculinity", or "new, modern man" as the alternative to the hegemonic traditional masculinity (Qambela, 2023; Musariri, 2021).[46] Musariri (2021:79) argues that these single stories leave no room for the nuance and abundance of masculinities that are often silenced by the volume and popularity of these totalizing claims. The "positive, new South African man", for example, is cast as an introspective man who, stereotypically, has no place in cultures of competitive team sports. The players who began speaking to me about mental health made their living from competitive football. Their masculinities were shifting and drew from certain aspects of both stereotyped masculine prototypes, going beyond these static representations. This is true for men in other homosocial institutions, such as prisons, where a combination of legitimacies and ideas of stereotyped masculinities are employed in the pursuit of certain goals (Moolman, 2017). Masculinities emerge based on the contexts of their production and various competing influences. The "traditional" man, or the

[46] This new man is sometimes framed in response to post-apartheid literature on the new, free, business-driven South African woman with complete autonomy over her body and sexuality (Gqola, 2018). It represents a clean rupture from the past and an uncritical embrace of neoliberal policies and global North imaginings of freedom and individuality that are translated to the "rainbow nation" that South Africa is often marketed as (Gqola, 2018; Qambela, 2023).

"man in crisis", or even the "modern man", fail to accurately represent the nuance and conflicting pressures placed upon the young sportsman in 2023. For example, DFC players would emphasize keeping their minds healthy when giving training advice, and would give feedback in games with a focus on positivity. When players addressed concerns to the wider group, the group seemed receptive and listened patiently.

In the contemporary moment, black hegemonic masculinities at DFC seemed to be relatively open on the matter of expression and mental health. In fact, after I had presented my initial proposal for interviews and observation at DFC, Coach Ash encouraged his players to speak to me in order "better understand ourselves" as men. "Soms is dit moeilik om te praat[47]", he reflected, as he welcomed me to the team. He urged the players to participate in the research project. This was the hierarchical leader of the club, its founder and chief selector, encouraging the players to learn about themselves and speak about the issues they faced. While some players felt that the sports club was *not* the place to discuss one's affective health, the general openness to the nature of such conversations within the wider club show the need for acknowledging incompleteness in Anthropological understandings of masculinities. The club facilitated three noticeable spheres of influence, identified by the players, which helped combat negative mental health amongst its men.

---

47 Translation: "Sometimes it's difficult to talk [about our problems]".

Religion in Upington

Each club prayed before and after training sessions and games. It was a regular and important ritual. These prayers would take place in a circle. Players interlocked arms, bowed their heads and displayed a quiet reverence. Prayer is perhaps more easily categorised as a divinatory ritual. It is used to petition God, the ultimate authority, for blessings and protection, and social success in many sporting milieus (Turner, 1973:1100). Set in a country where significant missionary activity accompanied colonial expansion (Comaroff and Comaroff, 1986), Upington is immersed in religious movement and practice. Upington is predominantly Christian. As of 2016, more than 95% of people in the Northern Cape identified as Christians (statsa.gov.za, 2016). In fact, much of its first geographical appearances in written historical archives locate it as a former mission station led by the aptly named, Reverend Christian Schroder (Legassick, 2016). Out of all the players I spoke to at both clubs, almost all believed in a single creator God despite differing levels of religious fervour.

Mali, the striker for Upington City, was a Muslim man from Mitchell's Plain in Cape Town who also took part in every prayer session. He was cautious to delve into religious conversation. "My religion is very personal", he said seriously. He believed it was important to pray in order to humble his own ego and sense of pride. He also mentioned his reliance on "the Almighty" to protect his children, who lived in an area of the country rife with gangsterism and public violence. The coaches were all committed Protestant Christians. They espoused some of the core values of Protestant Christianity such as discipline and self-sacrifice, a feature not uncommon to sports clubs in

Africa where "Muscular masculinities" thrive (Kovač, 2022:25). The sports clubs I worked with in Upington, therefore, promoted religious practices within its spaces through ritual, particularly through a Protestant lens.

Stability When the World Crumbles

In the sports club, religion helps players make sense of their realities. When I asked Shabba what it meant to be a man and how he had changed since joining the football club, he paused. He wanted to gather his thoughts. He began sharing an anecdote. Two years ago, he had received devastating news. His younger sister had died. The news of her passing catapulted him into waves of grief and existential angst. This introduces one of the fundamental benefits and uses of religion, especially for young black men in a precarious landscape. Religion often provides a sense of clarity. It is argued that the ritual performances that people adhere to are a part of their own attempts at theorizing reality (Deflem, 1991). Much of the grief Shabba was experiencing stemmed from his many unanswered questions. "Why did his sister have to die at such a young age? Why isn't life fair?" Religion and many other systems of thought have, as part of its basic aims, to explain and predict the events of things in the world (Deflem, 1991:12). In his confusion, religion was not Shabba's go-to form of comfort.

He was not particularly religious growing up. It was a combination of a failure of alternative coping mechanisms and the concern of his friends within the team that brought Shabba to religion. After weeks of growing resentment, Shabba had become a loose cannon, ready to rage and become violent at the slightest inconvenience. Anger, it seemed to him at the time, was the only way he could express his tumultuous mental state. His football suffered. Worse, he could feel himself become alienated by the club and wider friendship community because of his hot streak. At one of his lowest points, he was introduced to the Christian Revival Church, a charismatic Pentecostal movement which is particularly popular in Upington and has branches throughout South Africa. CRC has been recognized through official club forums as a positive influence on its players[48]. Shabba began attending homecell meetings with other young people. As he accepted the teachings and values of Protestant Christianity, he began to feel his anger dissipate. He could now ask his questions and felt free from judgment in a zone of sociality that encouraged vulnerability while maintaining youthful energy and camaraderie.

While we never covered the answers he received to his questions in the aftermath of his sister's passing, he feels comforted by his identity as a Christian and the "family" dynamic his religion allows him to access. Religion, like handshakes, are important rituals which facilitate social co-dependence and a period of social sameness and cooperation, or communitas (Turner, 1969). Religion, however, is unique from handshakes at Upington sports clubs in its provision of ontological value (Deflem, 1991:13). While handshakes represent recognition of sociality and value between club members, religion provides ontological value and identity for players beyond the realm of the sports

---

[48] They have been featured on the club's Instagram page as recently as August 2023. The two organizations have also collaborated on community projects in the past (via Facebook).

club, making it an attractively stable proposition for players whose sporting identities are always in flux.

Activation Opportunities in South African Football

Masculine identities within the sports club are often strongly based on financial security and the ability to provide for their families and dependants, especially given the opportunities for excess and the activation of stardom in sports. At Upington City, many of the mental health challenges faced by its players were directly proportional to their economic situations once they had become professional. This is a phenomenon that is common to many young men living in areas of economic precarity (Kovač, 2022:13). Uroš Kovač (2022:13) argues that the precarity of masculinity cannot be separated from the conditions which limit and expand their means of economic production. Many men are expected to be the breadwinners for their family (Kovač, 2022). Their heavily gendered success is based on financial provision.

Sport, especially at the highest level - can be a means of exponential masculine success, complemented with money, adoring fans, social stardom, sexual opportunity and a dramatic boost in happiness - the key factor in a healthy mind for almost half of the participants I spoke to. At Upington City, the players were employed by the club. DFC, meanwhile, was an amateur rugby club, where players would pay a fee to play. When I began observing and asking for interviews, Sithe, the club physiotherapist and my "inside man", began referring me to the club's most senior players - believing that they had the most to offer me in terms of wisdom and critical information on being a man in a sports club in Upington. Of the four senior players I interviewed, three were in their mid to late thirties. In the professional lifespan of a footballer, this was seniority. All four players had played at the highest level of South African football, the Premier Soccer League.

Professional football in South Africa is lucrative, especially in relation to other African countries with more footballing prestige. [49] In many African countries, opportunities for financial emancipation through sport is a tightly contested and often one-shot-only experience (Kovač, 2021, and Mfecane, 2018). In South Africa, however, players are often not required to leave the country to thrive financially because of lucrative professionalisation of sports clubs (Darby and Solberg, 2013). In the aftermath of Apartheid, and the ushering in of a competitive local league in the Premier Soccer League (established in 1996), companies saw professional football as a major marketing opportunity, a stance only enhanced by South Africa's hosting of the 2010 FIFA World Cup (Darby and Solberg, 2013:119).[50] Additionally, 27 out of South Africa's 36-man squad (75%) are based at domestic clubs as of 2023 (safa.net, 2023). This is, for example, a massive contrast to the 2 out of 26 players representing Ghana at the 2022 World Cup, who were based domestically (less than

---

[49] For example, countries such as Egypt, who boast more AFCON – African Cup of Nations – wins and have more African Champions League winners amongst their domestic clubs.

[50] ABSA Bank signed a R500 million naming rights deal with the league, followed by a R1.5 billion TV rights deal with Multichoice SuperSport.

8%). These lucrative potentials play into masculinities in the South African footballing context.

Approved: Financial Activation, Happiness and the Good Life

Scarra, the club captain, spoke of his first pay check with a disbelieving laugh, "it was like all my dreams were coming true". He had signed his first professional contract with Chippa United, a reputable team at the highest level of South African football. He was twenty-three years old. Leaving his hometown of George at the encouragement of his friends, and to the dismay of his family, he had moved to Cape Town to pursue professional football. His family were not happy that he had resigned from his work at a local fish factory. When Scarra first arrived in Cape Town, he stayed on his friend's couch in the poverty-stricken township of Samora Machel. Soon, he had made the big time. He remembers handing his bank card to his mother. They would be taken care of. They began physically seeing him thrive in what they had deemed an unpredictable career field. Chippa United's cup games were broadcast on one of South Africa's most accessible television broadcasting stations, SABC 1. His face brightened when he reminisced about the call he received from his family. They were filled with pride. They had seen their son and brother on the field through their screens. "I was young", Scarra continued, "and when you're young you don't see the traps around you".

Everybody wanted to be his friend. Oblivious to the intentions of his new friends, Scarra began lavishly spending at parties, showering his friends in the offerings of the "good life", and drinking excessively. He was thrilled. He was *the man.* The upward trajectory of his new sporting success did not last. After almost five years at the pinnacle of South African football, Scarra found himself without a club. His finances dwindled. His new friends were nowhere to be found. His family could no longer rely on his support. Scarra's mental health plummeted. Without a club and the material benefits that professional football offered, Scarra became increasingly anxious and would find himself in a near-constant state of depression and sadness. He had been betrayed. The economic stability which had propped up his (in his words) "ego" and had convinced him that he was *the* complete, social and healthy man had now been ripped out from under his feet. He had become a victim of a cruel, illusionary form of optimism (Berlant, 2020). This reflects Kovač's (2022) belief that sporting masculinities, especially amongst those aspiring to professional stardom, are keenly linked to the financial agency of players.

"The Only One Left": Fashioning the Self from the Other

Loyal friendship in external communities and kinship and mentorship inside club spaces provided an invaluable antidote to the precarious performances of masculine stardom. Many players told how their "youthful bravado" crumbled in the face of financial precarity. While I chose to highlight Scarra's story because of the depth of our almost three-hour interview, his' is not a solitary experience. All of the senior players I interviewed at Upington City reflected on similar trajectories and ego-based masculine happiness which left - along with previously sycophantic dependants disguised as friends - when their material success diminished.

For Mali, the club's tall striker, his lowest mental point was also a part of "becoming a man". When I asked what that experience was like, he had no hesitation to share.

> It was hard. I felt like no-one cared about me, only my wife. She was the only one left. Then I started realizing what it is to be a man. Before, I only thought about myself, what I wanted, showing off and impressing my friends at different [night]clubs. I was a boy. My wife was there for me when no-one else was. So now I have to show her that I'm there for her when she needs me.

Mali's mental wellbeing and idea of self was no longer predicated on immediate financial gratification or the need to impress others with his riches. This does not mean that material success no longer influenced Mali's mental health. He had joined Upington City motivated by the possibility of a better life for his kids, who live in an area rife with criminal activity and potential danger. "I'm much happier now. I don't live for me anymore", he concluded. In the light of financial and gendered failure, interdependence and interconnectivity emerged as a key measure for improving the mental health of men in the sports club.

What's Love Got to Do With It?

The affective health of men at the sports club are intrinsically linked to the ways in which they are acknowledged and cared for by others. Different forms of care position the self in relation to others (Musariri, 2021). Affective, or mental health, and the tensions between interconnectivity and autonomy are soothed by caregiving practices which demonstrate the value placed on the individual and their needs, while offering belonging to a wider group. These care practices often create a tangible awareness of interconnectivity and the ways in which humans depend on one another to thrive. Mali recognised that he would be forever indebted to his wife, who cared for him in his lowest moments. This activated a new expression of masculine identity for him, where his affective health was hinged on the wellbeing of his kinship units and no longer an isolated project. Nyamnjoh (2022:596) theorises this phenomenon in his work on *Citizenship, Incompleteness and Mobility:* "When one borrows and acknowledges the fact of being in the debt of others, one cultivates a sense of who one is through others, and by so doing de-essentializes who one is."

My experiences in the field seemed to buttress my belief that men[51] need love in order to practice healthy affective masculinities. Ratele (2022:24) describes men's need for love as a growth need, a dependency on others to recognize and activate one's talents and validate existence. Men and masculinities are embedded in dominant patriarchal cultures which often downplay their love needs (Ratele, 2022). Where autonomy and an individual notion of manhood are prioritised, the man lives purely to suit his own ends, and he suffers (Mauss, 1950:75). Consistently in senior player testimonies, their lowest affective moments were triggered by the realization that the "love" they had received from footballing success and its subsequent material activation, was conditional. This was devastating.

[51] And certainly not only men.

Mali and Scarra spoke of the demoralizing self-doubt and lack of belief in their own autonomy if football would not work out. Ironically, this identity crisis and depression was strongly linked to the realization that those they had depended on to fuel their ego and enable their self-made status, had been leaching on them in parasitic exchanges, as opposed to a mutual interdependence in debt and indebtedness. Men exposed to webs of conditional love, often embrace deleterious behaviours in reaction to the suffering and wretchedness of such experiences (Ratele, 2022:25). The mental health of men in the sports club is intimately tied to player perceptions of the care and interdependence they have with others.

Brother to Brother: Conversational Care

The clubhouse was a place where love and care functioned as a result of the closeness between club members who fashioned new kinship relationships in Upington. Caring masculinities should be viewed in relation to the structures which enable and restrict care and its forms (Ratele, 2022:38). While kinship structures reinforce the kinds of motivations and goals - like familial provision or stardom - that are at play within sports club participation, kinship itself is made possible through certain club functions. Manderson and Block (2016:205) argue that the quality of kinship structures are manifested in the types of care provided between kin. The relationships surrounding these new kinship structures are often therapeutic (Ratele, 2022:45). They allow men to speak about the concerns they face (Ratele, 2022).

Conversations matter. This was perhaps best exemplified in Alex's emotional backstory, which he revealed to me during a deep conversation at a local coffee shop. His brother had recently committed suicide. His brother, who had once stabbed Alex after an altercation, had according to Alex, never regularly spoken to anyone on a deep level. Growing up in a home rife with social problems, he was shy and antisocial. He became a recluse after high school. Alex reflected, "If you don't have anyone to speak to, you go crazy… I wish he would've spoken to me". All the participants I interviewed characterized their closest relationships (both in and outside of the sports club) around the opportunity for conversation. They spoke of the ability to speak freely about a plethora of often intimate issues.

For Thabiso, a short and contemplative young man, the biggest boost to his mental health was the openness of discussion within the clubhouse. "We are all athletes, but first we're people. The boys [his teammates] help each other with anything. Most of us live here [the clubhouse] and it feels like a family." While Thabiso admitted that he could not speak to every player about all of the challenges he dealt with, he claimed to have a special bond with two teammates, with whom he would often go on walks and confide in. "Those guys are my brothers", Thabiso concluded. "Brothers" was a term which exemplified Thabiso's understanding of the kinship bonds at the club. Care was evident. In my time at the clubhouse, I witnessed close camaraderie between players, who often cut each other's hair, played ludo together on a makeshift board, told jokes or carried ice to make ice baths after training in the scorching sun. The players seemed on good terms with the female kitchen staff too, and gathered in the mornings and afternoons for group meals. The relationships forged as a result of clubhouse dynamics and openness to conversation were beneficial to the affective health of the young men who made up Upington City FC. It was evidence of ubuntu in action – a person is a person through others.

One-for-All: Finding Identity through Relatability, Histories and Duty

The closeness between Upington City's players was enhanced by the intricate interweaving between their conceptions of the self in relation to their similar goals, backgrounds and obligations they felt towards team-building and interconnectivity. Their close physical proximity and the need for respect in stabilising the dynamics necessary for co-living at the clubhouse, helped facilitate affectionate relationships amongst young men at the club. However, beyond basic politeness, the idea of team identity was crucial to understanding and fashioning the self. This was key to player identities, both in the sports club and in the communities out of which they emerged. The club employs players who are often similar in age. At Upington City, many of the players undergo relatable experiences. Fundamentally, all of them aspire to be part of a winning and ambitious football team and to be winning players with upwardly mobile footballing trajectories. This common goal allows players to "sacrifice for the team[52]". Kovač (2022:154) concluded his study on the precarity of masculinity in

---

[52] Shabba describing putting his ego aside (after coach Nkosi berated him for his decision-making on the field earlier that day) to do his best for the team.

football clubs by claiming that "young men [in sports clubs] show an incredible capacity to aspire".[53]

Many also share similar struggles. Two major social groups became evidently visible during my time there. One group was made up of players from Upington. Many of them had grown up in the same *lokasie*, an Afrikaans term meaning "hood" or "ghetto". The second group was made up of younger players who had moved to Upington from other parts of South Africa, many of whom were experiencing their first or second stints of life away from home. The two players I had interviewed from this group both referred to their home communities as *kasi*, a derivative of *lokasie* denoting being from a predominantly Black township on the outskirts of major South African cities, a result of Apartheid planning and spatial racism in South Africa (Mohamed, 2023:132). Being from similar class, racial or geographical backgrounds often makes establishing ties with others at workplaces much easier (Rezende, 2020:90). The players from Upington itself would walk to their various homes as a group after training. Those from outside of Upington would get into the bus headed for the clubhouse.

Players chose to be close even outside of club proximities, a functional friendship enabled through the club as a social frontier. On more than one occasion, I ran into small groups of players running errands together at the local mall. These young men

53 The shared aspirations to reach the pinnacle of South African Football have begun to materialize for Upington City, who won in their regional, and then national playoffs to reach the Motsepe Championship, just one level below the Premier Soccer League. As of November 2024, they have a very realistic chance of promotion at the end of the current season.

found joy and companionship in shared duty. Outside of the club, the family unit was operationalized as another team which made the self. Both being a man in the family, and a man in the sports club, were intimately connected to duty. Adherence to these shared duties are often ways in which love is expressed, and affective health is attended to (Ratele, 2022:51).

Friendships of Duty?

James G. Carrier, in *the Anthropology of Friendship* (2020), conceptualises friendships as a voluntary social phenomenon where each party is "free" to bestow gifts (in various forms) on the other without an expectation of compensation. Being "unconstrained" is the defining feature of a friend, which he differentiates from kin, colleagues or patrons (Carrier, 2020). This, he admits (2020:21), is an uncompromising view of friendship, emerging out of a liberal Western discourse which prioritises individuality.

Anthropologist Sakhumzi Mfecane (2018) argues for African-centred approaches for discussing masculinities and the social worlds in which they are manifested. He argues that while the individual is an agent in masculine production, they are tied up in a larger composite understanding of what it means to be human through interconnections with others and the environment (Mfecane, 2018:295). Carrier, meanwhile, also creates firm boundaries between friendships and convenient relationships, based on the notion of attractiveness. Players at Upington City and DFC did not often speak about attractiveness or the qualities in their teammates that enabled the friendship. While this may be linked to the fear of association with homosociality (as discussed in Chapter 5), the players also highlighted the qualities of the relationship as central to their friendships, and their own masculinities. This reflects the importance of Mfecane's (2018) plea to use African-centred theories to understand the links between masculine constructions and friendship through obligation and world-making with those around them.

It was in the best interest of the self – as an individual and community product – to forge friendships of "convenience". The affective health of the self-falters when one is not part of the team. Regardless of whether or not the young men at Upington City and DFC were attracted to their wives[54] and their teammates, they were a part of the team, and the team was a part of them.[55] The friendships formed as a result of the bonds of space, aspirations, goals, relatability and intersubjective vulnerabilities therefore emerged as a key part of theorising the self, and maintaining affective health for young men in Upington's sports clubs.

---

[54] I am **not** claiming that players are not attracted to their wives. I am, rather, asserting that attraction is not the only reason for the success of the friendship/relationship in constructing self and affirming affective health.

[55] Obligations, here, should not be confused with conditional love. These obligations help facilitate interconnectivity which shapes the affective health of the self. Both parties remain obligated to one another, even when one does not live up to that obligation e.g., in the story of Mali, whose wife remained by his side even when he had little in terms of materiality to offer her. Conditional love, meanwhile, damages the individual who has been used as a mine for personal use. Instead of interconnectivity, the dependants have leached off their supposed friend, and abandon him once he has no more left to satiate their greed.

Belief as Activation: A Nod from the Uncle

Mentorship emerged as another way in which affective health is regulated and maintained in sports clubs in Upington. Unlike the more visibilised performances of religious ritual and practice, or the more explicit, verbally acknowledged, bonds of kinship and friendship, mentorship was more subtle practice. I had enquired about male role models in the lives of the young men at the club. This was based on my own understandings of my father as a role model who was an early example of the parameters and possibilities of being a man, in my life.

Anthropologists on masculinities have argued that the supportive presence of an adult male in the life of a child can have a beneficial impact on its activation and a relieving effect on women, often burdened with the task of single parenthood (Morrell and Richter 2006). This does not have to involve a man who is biologically related. In South Africa, maternal or paternal uncles, grandfathers, stepfathers, older male neighbours, or teachers often become fathers in the sense of male models to be emulated by boys and young men (Clowes, Ratele, and Shefer 2013). Hans Reihling, in his excellent work on the emotional side of masculinities, went as far as to claim, "affective health depended on the kind of relationship men established with male role models." (Reihling, 2022:41). Tien, of DFC, had a complex relationship with his father, whom he saw as a taskmaster. His own father's harsh strictness and reified ideas about what it meant to be man, had a telling effect on his affective practices. "I will talk to my mom here and there [about my feelings] but never my dad. He expects [my brother and I] to be strong. It's easier to talk to girls [about my feelings]."

While he believed that addressing mental health was important, he felt more confident doing so in the company of the women in his life. For many of the Upington City players meanwhile, they had no present father figure, but were often "adopted" by their uncles, friends and community members. These mentors had often supported their childhood dreams for footballing activation. Scarra was given a R2000 to travel to Cape Town by a group of uncles who believed in his talent and dedication. Mali, meanwhile, credited a local "Uncle" who would transport kids to a local field every Saturday to participate in football tournaments. "He was there every Saturday. He let me get on the *bakkie*[56] even though he knew I was too small [to participate in the age-group categorized leagues]." These mentors had shown belief in the young boys under their care and facilitated their masculine sporting dreams, dreams which had remarkably come true. Its remarkability is based on the precarity of professional sports (Kovač, 2022).

While of course, not all stories of mentorship are wholesome and contribute to activation and healthy affect in boys, the stories I received from club members never revealed any misconduct. Such matters are sensitive, and often deeply private. I do not want to speculate, however, based on data I do not have, and choose rather to work with the narratives presented to me by the players, who generally speak positively of their present male role models.

---

[56] Pickup Truck

A Word from the Wise

For the senior players I had interviewed, some found mentorship to be a manner of reciprocating the gifts of the male role models who had helped activate them. These players, who had traversed the ups-and-downs of South African football, and were probably approaching the twilight of their careers (Scarra was thirty-seven), wanted to guide the young men in the team. They see themselves as positive figures who the younger players can learn from. Ironically, when I brought up mentorship in the club, the young Thabiso laughed. "Scarra told you his whole life story ne?", he grinned. "Yeah, we [the young players] hear it a lot. Yoh, every time." It seemed Scarra's mentorship had become a humorous in-joke amongst the players who now jokingly pretended to avoid asking him questions so as not to be subject to a retelling of his narrated autobiography. "He means well though, and we know if we're struggling with anything, we can go to him. Besides, that guy played in the PSL (Premier Soccer League) for years!" Mentorship kept the avenues for conversation open. In addition, Scarra's exploits on the field gave him an air of reverence amongst the aspiring footballers. Young footballers often look up to role models who have achieved what they one day dream of, as evidence that their aspirations have credibility (Kovač, 2022).

Additionally, many of the young players felt that Scarra was wise, and could give them advice that would facilitate their own careers. More than the attainment of football skills, young men often follow the behaviour examples of senior professionals through tenets like discipline, hard work and discernment (Kovač, 2022:90). The senior players were once younger men too. They seemed balanced when sharing the advice they give. "You are still young so it's natural to want to experience [the good] life, but we make sure they know that it's not real. That's not where you find your *real* friends (Shabba, 2023)." While boredom seems to be a typical phenomenon in the "free" time players have at Upington City, Thabiso's responses to questions about clubbing and the night life seemed to consistently close it off as a viable leisure activity. "Our body is our job. Besides, there's nothing good [for my future] at the clubs." These kinds of internalized narratives show how mentorship impacts the masculinities on display at sports clubs through examples and cautionary advice, while providing players with avenues for conversation about affect. Through religious activity, friendship and kinship relations and mentorship, young men in Upington sports clubs navigate affective health more easily. The interconnectivity that the club enables, in turn helps players navigate their own multiple identities and be more autonomous through the relationships which activate them.

"For Women Only": Alternative Perspectives from the Club

Not everyone at the club believed the dominant narrative presented in this chapter. For some, the club was not a space to speak about mental health. Regan's perspectives on mental health were a stark contrast to those presented by Upington City and DFC players during the interview process. He was a player at the rugby club. Our conversation took place in his car as we drove home. I asked if he felt that being socialised as a man in Upington meant it was more difficult to speak about one's mental health. I had barely finished my sentence before he made a disclaimer.

> "Let me be honest with you, I don't believe in all that mental health stuff. For a woman, I can understand. But when a man talks about mental health?", he pulled a face akin to expressing disgust. "The problem is, our generation of men are soft. We don't want to work, don't want to do things for ourselves. The easy option is to complain about your "mental health", but the reality is that most of them are soft or lazy. Men should never speak about mental health."

Regan was heavily self-reliant. He was the only player at DFC that I had known prior to the observation periods in January and June. I consider him a lifelong friend. He had been taking care of his mother since before we met at the end of my high school years. He was kind and friendly, and we had developed a good relationship. I also knew that he had big dreams of financial activation and starting a family. Regan's answer to my question reflected a shift in the narratives about the positive influence of the social connections at the sports club on men's mental health. It denied mental health as a viable topic of discussion for valuable and ambitious men. This shows incompleteness in the way mental health and affective masculinities are discussed in the sports club.

While Coach Ash attributes the lack of openness and vulnerability to the socialisation of young men and their fear of being regarded as soft, Regan provides an interesting alternative worldview. In the pursuit of his dreams, attending to questions about mental health is regarded as a pathway to laziness. In the unrelenting drive to find his own sense of fulfilment through hard work, Regan sees affective masculinities as a break from tradition that allows men to escape responsibilities and justify their own stagnation. While I disagreed with him, I respected his opinion on the matter. His viewpoint may have contributed to the statement made by Alex in Chapter 6, who admitted that he did not believe his problems were worth mentioning in front of the wider group of players.

Talking through mental health with participants once again revealed to me the complexities of different positionalities and systems of socialisation at play within the sports club frontier. It revealed the importance of leaving room for incompleteness when subscribing to a certain narrative within sports clubs. The contrasting notions of mental health amongst young men within the club exemplifies the "dynamic struggle" between autonomy and interconnectivity in men's affective health. It also shows a general movement away from stigmatised and static notions of gendered care, while highlighting the real influence of these stigmas in Regan's dismissal of mental health as a topic of conversation for men.

Conclusion

Ultimately, there was a general trend towards the acknowledgement of the importance of addressing men's mental health and the provision of certain social tools within the sports club to help address this. Theories about *toxic masculinity* have presented single narratives which have often overlooked men's struggles with affective health. This absence has been reinforced by the alternative means of expression utilized by many black, heterosexual men, who have avoided clinics and public forums for openness. The sports club had a more positive effect on the affect of its participants.

Mental health was a narrative that emerged out of the interview discussions. Participants, especially at Upington City, were keen to speak about their own journeys with mental health, often closely linking it to their interconnective practices with others. Three main club structures stood out as an aid in the mental health of its men. Religious ritual and belief emerged as a powerful ontological tool for young men in the sports club. Friendship and kinship through mutual aspirations emerged as another way of self-making and affective growth, especially in the wake of falls from stardom and the harsh realities of conditional forms of love. Finally, mentorship emerged as another tool to build affective health through advice and open dialogue. These club structures facilitated interconnections which proved invaluable to the mental health of many players. Despite this overall trend, a single story about the influence of the sports club on men's mental health ignores the nuances and different perspectives that are found within club structures. It is therefore important for Anthropologists to acknowledge these different tensions and be eager to listen for narratives outside of the "grain", the dominant narrative of mental health that presented itself in my interviews. Regan's perspective reflects the different discourses about affective masculinities that persist in Upington's sports clubs, each motivated by different and similar personal life experiences and wider systems of socialisation.

Chapter 8

Conclusion

Recapitulation of Research Objectives

To investigate how sports clubs influenced performances and conceptions of masculinities in the town of Upington, South Africa, I worked with a rugby and football club respectively over a combined seven-week period. Gender is important for influencing permissible behaviours within shifting cultural boundaries. Masculinities cannot be separated from their intersections with other categories of identities and the lived experiences that shape its embodiment. When problematising masculinities, popular media and academic narratives in South Africa have tended to theorise Black masculinities between the poles of victims of structural violence and precarity, and perpetrators of hegemonic violence over women, queer groups and othered masculinities. This book, using the framework of incompleteness, gathered perspectives from inside the sports club to shed light on the experiences and nuances of Black masculinities and its various iterations in Upington. Sports clubs are valuable sites of analyses due to their popularity and colonial history as a means of moralizing leisure time for Black men in South Africa. It is an important institution for negotiating passage into manhood for many boys. The club serves as a frontier and an agent for masculine ideals and different masculinities located at various intersections of identity which shape and are shaped by the club and its members.

Research Findings

The sports club placed emphasis on understanding and executing responsibility as a precursor for activation as a valued man. The club, made up of different sites, presented players with opportunities for specialised responsibilities according to the social norms and encounters present in each site. Meeting these responsibilities were an important part of negotiating higher status amongst peers and elders within the social structure. While part of this specialised responsibility was the upkeep of the body as a sporting machine through training, sporting masculinities also included responsibilities towards team-building, community and care. Lift-clubs were a prime example of this. The club was also a moralizing force, with messages aimed at Black and Coloured[57] masculinities in particular, encouraging ambitious pursuit of goals and freedom from vices and juvenile delinquency. The Black masculinities at the club were dominated by heterosexual framing, and othered sexualities were hidden behind jokes and unserious conversation. Ableism and class dynamics created perceptual dichotomies between effeminised, "soft" men, and their idealised "hard" counterparts. Intersectional views of masculinities in the sports club revealed complex and co-existing ideals, where players' own histories and subjectivities determine what is permissible in a club structure that does not necessarily reproduce polarising masculine tropes.

The complexity of these encounters were demonstrated in handshake rituals, which both reinforced social hierarchies and made room for the

---

[57] Which falls under the Biko definition of blackness, although it was imagined differently – and provided different affordances – under the Apartheid racial classificatory system.

possibility of new relationships and dynamics. Handshakes also reintroduced appropriate, heterosocial forms of care and recognition which were suspended during the physicality of rugby. During the research period, the tragic death of two players on the field rocked the club and brought a halt to amateur rugby in the region. In the aftermath, players revealed that enjoyment of rugby was one of the fundamental reasons why they play. In addition, they felt as though the club was not the place to reveal sensitive emotions. The club, however, provide platforms for other forms of expression and showed care through the implementation of an emergency medical fund. This reveals the complexity of permissible masculinities in the club setting, and also the genuine joy that the club adds to player leisure. In addition, it positions the players as people in addition to what they can offer the club. The club, like its players, is incomplete and is activated by drawing on group dynamics and a variety of subjective masculinities, which regulate and are regulated by the club.

One of the most important aspects of player life regulated heavily by club structures is affective health. Rather than focusing on biophysical or medical models of mental health, this paper focused on wellbeing from player perspectives. Since the rise of social media and the problematising of toxic and stagnant approaches to masculinities, gender expression in the realm of affect has become more malleable in the lives of participants. They expressed affective health as a particularly masculine challenge that the sports clubs help to manage, mainly through religion, friendship and mentoring respectively. Religion, and its ritual practices that are maintained within and outside of the club have provided some players with ontological stability. Friendships of obligation, and the revelation of cruel optimisms through previous interactions with sycophants helped many realise how important interconnectivity was to their masculine performance. Finally, the clubs unofficially embark on mentoring systems where players are activated through their proximity and adherence to advice from senior players in different phases of their gendered development. Not all players believed affective health was an important or necessary talking point for men, revealing incompleteness even within generally accepted destigmatisation and narratives about openness and vulnerability.

Suggestions towards Future Research

Future research on the topic of masculinities through the lens of sports clubs will benefit from a more focused and concerted effort at one particular sport or level of play e.g., amateur clubs in Upington, or rugby clubs in Upington. More time in the field would also enhance this research and allow for longer and perhaps more engaging relationships with club members. In addition, this book excludes explicit experiences and perspectives from women, queer groups, and masculinities not associated with the sporting ideals of the club. Future research would benefit from a deeper integration into the communities where sports clubs are created and held. Incompleteness is a life-changing framework that should be strongly considered by future Anthropologists who will do important work in developing the canon in the Critical Study of Men and Masculinities. This book is a valiant, necessary and incomplete lens on masculinities through the lens of sports clubs. I hope it sheds important light on a town, gender category, and fundamental social structures that mean so much to me and others. May it contribute to future scholarship in these regions that shape South Africa and the academy towards acknowledging incompleteness and the need for convivial, messy and constantly negotiated relationships.

Reference

Ammann, C. and Staudacher, S., 2021. Masculinities in Africa beyond crisis: complexity, fluidity, and intersectionality. *Gender, Place & Culture*, *28*(6), pp.759-768.

Anderson, C.M., Bielert, T.A. and Jones, R.P., 2004. One country, one sport, endless knowledge: The anthropological study of sports in South Africa. *Anthropologica*, pp.47-55.

Anderson, E.D., 2009. The maintenance of masculinity among the stakeholders of sport. Sport management review, 12(1), pp.3-14.

Anthropology Southern Africa. (2005). Ethical guidelines and principles of conduct for anthropologists. *Anthropology Southern Africa*, *28*(3-4), 142-143.

Bantjes, J., Kagee, A. and Meissner, B., 2017. Young men in post-apartheid South Africa talk about masculinity and suicide prevention. South African journal of psychology, 47(2), pp.233-245.

Behar, R. 1996. *The Vulnerable Observer: Anthropology That Breaks Your Heart.* Boston, MA: Beacon Press.

Berlant, L., 2020. *Cruel optimism.* Duke University Press.

Besnier, N., Brownell, S. and Carter, T.F., 2018. *The anthropology of sport: Bodies, borders, biopolitics.* University of California Press.

Besnier, N. and Brownell, S., 2012. Sport, modernity, and the body. *Annual Review of Anthropology*, *41*, pp.443-459.

Besnier, N., Guinness, D., Hann, M. and Kovač, U., 2018. Rethinking masculinity in the neoliberal order: Cameroonian footballers, Fijian rugby players, and Senegalese wrestlers. *Comparative Studies in Society and History*, *60*(4), pp.839-872.

Bhana, D., and Mayeza, E. 2016. "'We Don't Play with Gays, They're Not Real Boys … They Can't Fight': Hegemonic Masculinity and (Homophobic) Violence in the Primary Years of Schooling." International Journal of Educational Development 51, 36–42.

Bhana, D., 2008. 'Six packs and big muscles, and stuff like that'. Primary school-aged South African boys, black and white, on sport. *British Journal of Sociology of Education*, *29*(1), pp.3-14.

Bogopa, D., 2001. Sports Development: Obstacles and Solutions in South Africa. *African Anthropologist*, *8*(1), pp.85-95.

Bourdieu, P., 1990. *The logic of practice*. Stanford university press.

Boulton, J., 2023. Beyond Toxic Masculinity: Reading and Writing Men in Post-Apartheid Namibia. *Africa Spectrum*, p.00020397231175170.

Breckenridge, K., 1998. The allure of violence: Men, race and masculinity on the South African goldmines, 1900–1950. *Journal of Southern African Studies*, *24*(4), pp.669-693.

Butler, J., 2016. Performative Acts and Gender Constitution: An Essay in Phenomenology and Feminist Theory. Theater Journal, 40 (4).

Carrier, J.G., 2020. People who can be friends: Selves and social relationships. In The anthropology of friendship (pp. 21-38). Routledge.

Clowes, L., Ratele, K. and Shefer, T., 2013. Who needs a father? South African men reflect on being fathered. Journal of gender studies, 22(3), pp.255-267.

Coetzee, E.L., Pelser, T.G., Ngwenya, B. and Prinsloo, J.J., 2021. Transformation of professional cricket, rugby and soccer in South Africa since 1994: A systematic review. *African Journal for Physical Activity and Health Sciences (AJPHES)*, *27*(2), pp.218-247.

Collins, P.H., 1986. Learning from the outsider within: The sociological significance of Black feminist thought. *Social problems*, *33*(6), pp.14-s32.

Comaroff, J. and Comaroff, J., 1986. Christianity and colonialism in South Africa. *American ethnologist*, 13(1), pp.1-22.

Connell, R.W. and Messerschmidt, J.W., 2005. Hegemonic masculinity: Rethinking the concept. *Gender & society*, *19*(6), pp.829-859.

Connell, R., 2006. Glass ceilings or gendered institutions? Mapping the gender regimes of public sector worksites. *Public administration review*, *66*(6), pp.837-849.

Darby, P. and Solberg, E., 2013. Differing trajectories: football development and patterns of player migration in South Africa and Ghana. In South Africa and the Global Game (pp. 118-130). Routledge.

Davis, L. (2017). Introduction: Disability, Normality and Power. In. Lennard Davis (ed.) *The Disability Studies Reader, 5th Edition* (pp. 1-14). Abingdon & New York: Routledge.

Deflem, M., 1991. Ritual, anti-structure, and religion: A discussion of Victor Turner's processual symbolic analysis. Journal for the scientific study of religion, pp.1-25.

Elliott, K., 2016. Caring masculinities: Theorizing an emerging concept. *Men and masculinities*, *19*(3), pp.240-259.

Fast, D., Bukusi, D. and Moyer, E., 2020. The knife's edge: Masculinities and precarity in East Africa. *Social Science & Medicine*, *258*, p.113097.

Fuh, D., 2012, December. The prestige economy: Veteran clubs and young men's competition in Bamenda, Cameroon. In Urban Forum (Vol. 23, No. 4, pp. 501-526). Dordrecht: Springer Netherlands.

Geertz, C., 1973. 'Thick description: Toward an interpretive theory of culture', in *The Interpretation of Cultures*. New York: Basic Books. pp. 3-30.

Goffman, E., 2009. *Relations in public.* Transaction Publishers.

Gqola, P.D., 2018. A peculiar place for a feminist? The New South African woman, True Love magazine and Lebo (gang) Mashile. In *Contemporary African Mediations of Affect and Access* (pp. 13-30). Routledge.

Gqola, P.D., 2007. How the 'cult of femininity' and violent masculinities support endemic gender based violence in contemporary South Africa. *African identities*, *5*(1), pp.111-124.

Hamilton, S.N., 2017. Rituals of intimate legal touch: regulating the end-of-game handshake in pandemic culture. *The Senses and Society*, *12*(1), pp.53-68.

hooks b (2004) The Will to Change: Men, Masculinity, and Love. New York: Atria Books.

Jewkes, R. K., Dunkle, K., Nduna, M., and Shai, N., 2010. 'Intimate Partner Violence, Relationship Power Inequity, and Incidence of HIV Infection in Young Women in South Africa: A Cohort Study.' *The Lancet* 376 (9734): 41–48. https://doi.org/10.1016/S0140-6736(10)60548-X.

ka Canham, H., 2023. *Riotous deathscapes.* Duke University Press.

Kovač, U., 2021. Becoming Useful and Humble: Masculinity, Morality, and Association Football in

Cameroon. *Anthropological Quarterly*, *94*(3), pp.411-442.

Kovač, U., 2022. *The precarity of masculinity: Football, Pentecostalism, and transnational aspirations in Cameroon*. Berghahn Books.

Kaur, T., 2016. Sporting lives and" development" agendas: a critical analysis of sport and" development" nexus in the context of farm workers of the Western Cape.

Keimbou, D.C.K., 2005. Games, Body and Culture: Emerging Issues in the Anthropology of Sport and Physical Education in Cameroon (1920-60). *International Review for the Sociology of Sport*, *40*(4), pp.447-466.

Kidd, B., 2013. Sports and masculinity. *Sport in society*, *16*(4), pp.553-564.

Legassick, M., 2016. Hidden Histories of Gordonia: Land dispossession and resistance in the Northern Cape, 1800–1990. NYU Press.

Magubane, B., 1963. *Sports and Politics in an Urban African Community-A Case Study of African Voluntary Organizations* (Doctoral book, University of Natal).

Malaby, T.M., 2009. Anthropology and play: The contours of playful experience. *New Literary History*, *40*(1), pp.205-218.

Manderson, L. and Block, E., 2016. Relatedness and care in Southern Africa and beyond. *Social Dynamics*, *42*(2), pp.205-217.

Mauss, M., 1973. Techniques of the Body. *Economy and society*, *2*(1), pp.70-88.

Mauss, M., 1950. The gift: The form and reason for exchange in primitive societies. *W. Halls (trans.) New York and London: WW Norton.*

Mead, M., 1977. Letters from the field: 1925-1975.

Mfecane, S., 2018. Towards African-centred theories of masculinity. *Social Dynamics*, *44*(2), pp.291-305.

Mfecane, S., 2020. Decolonising men and masculinities research in South Africa. *South African Review of Sociology*, *51*(2), pp.1-15.

Mohamed, K., 2023. Protesting death-disability-debility imaginaries: Ontological erasure and the endemic violences of settler colonialism.

Moolman, B., 2017. Negotiating masculinities and authority through intersecting discourses of tradition and modernity in South Africa. *Norma*, *12*(1), pp.38-47.

Moore, W., 2022. Boys Will be Boys, and Other Myths: Unravelling Biblical Masculinities. SCM Press.

Morgan, K.L., 2015. 'What Would They do if you Greeted?' The Potentiality of Greetings in the New South Africa. *African Studies*, *74*(1), pp.123-145.

Morrell, R., Jewkes, R. and Lindegger, G., 2012. Hegemonic masculinity/masculinities in South Africa: Culture, power, and gender politics. *Men and masculinities*, *15*(1), pp.11-30.

Morrell, R. and Swart, S., 2005. Men in the third world. *Handbook of studies on men and masculinities*, pp.90-113.

Morrell, R. 1998. 'Of Boys and Men: Masculinity and Gender in Southern African Studies.' *Journal of Southern African Studies* 24 (4): 605–30. https://doi.org/10.1080/03057079808708593.

Morrell, R., 2017. Touch rugby, masculinity and progressive politics in Durban, South Africa, 1985–1990. *The International Journal of the History of Sport*, *34*(7-8), pp.619-638.

Musariri, L. and Moyer, E., 2021. A black man is a cornered man: migration, precarity and masculinities in Johannesburg. *Gender, Place & Culture*, 28(6), pp.888-905.

Musariri, L., 2021. Becoming cornered: Migration, masculinities and marginalisation in inner-city Johannesburg.

Narayan, K., 1993. How native is a" native" anthropologist?. *American anthropologist, 95*(3), pp.671-686.

Nauright, J., 1998. *Sport, cultures, and identities in South Africa*. New Africa Books.

Newman, T.J., McCray, K., Lower-Hoppe, L.M., Rockhill, C., Ingram, D., Ohanasian, J. and Simmons-Horton, S., 2023. Healthy masculinity construction: The influence of race, faith and athletics. *Children & Society*, 37(3), pp.854-874.

Nyamnjoh, F.B., 2015. *C'est l'homme qui fait l'homme: Cul-de-Sac Ubuntu-ism in Cote d Ivoire*. Bamenda: Langaa.

Nyamnjoh, F.B., 2022. Citizenship, incompleteness and mobility. *Citizenship Studies, 26*(4-5), pp.592-598.

Nyamnjoh, F.B., 2024. Incompleteness as a framework for convivial scholarship and practice in healing. *Acta Academica, 56*(1), pp.121-147.

Nyamnjoh, F.B., 2017. Incompleteness: Frontier Africa and the currency of conviviality. *Journal of Asian and African studies, 52*(3), pp.253-270.

Nyamnjoh, F.B., 2012. 'Potted Plants in Greenhouses: A Critical Reflection on the Resilience of Colonial Education in Africa,' in: *Journal of Asian and African Studies,* Vol.47(2):129-154.

Nyamnjoh, F.B., 2016. *#RhodesMustFall: Nibbling at resilient colonialism in South Africa*. Bamenda: Langaa.

Oyěwùmí, O. (1997) *The invention of women making an African sense of Western gender discourses*. Minneapolis: University of Minnesota Press.

Qambela, G., 2023. "There is only one place for me. It is here, entabeni" Inxeba (2017), Kalushi (2016) and the difficulties of "the urban" for the New South African Man. In *Cinematic Imaginaries of the African City* (pp. 53-68). London: Routledge.

Peterson, J.B., 2018. *12 rules for life: An antidote to chaos.* Random House Canada.

Pratt, M.L., 1992. Science, planetary consciousness, interiors. *Imperial eyes: Travel writing and transculturation*, pp.15-37.

Ratele, K., 2016. *Liberating masculinities.* Cape Town: HSRC press.

Ratele, K., 2013. Masculinities without tradition. *Politikon*, *40*(1), pp.133-156.

Ratele, K., 2022. *Why men hurt women and other reflections on love, violence and masculinity.* NYU Press.

Ratele, K., 2015. Working through resistance in engaging boys and men towards gender equality and progressive masculinities. *Culture, Health & Sexuality*, *17*(sup2), pp.144-158.

Reihling, H., 2020. *Affective health and masculinities in South Africa: An ethnography of (in) vulnerability.* London: Routledge.

Renold, E. 2005. Girls, Boys and Junior Sexualities Exploring Children's Gender and Sexual Relations in the Primary School. New York: Routledge.

Rezende, C.B., 2020. Building affinity through friendship. In *The anthropology of friendship* (pp. 79-97). London: Routledge.

Richter, L. and Morrell, R., 2006. Baba: men and fatherhood in South Africa.

Robinson, V., 2004. Taking risks: Identity, masculinities and rock climbing. In *Understanding Lifestyle Sport* (pp. 125-142). Routledge.

Russell, B.H. (2006). Chapter 15. Direct and Indirect Observation, in *Research Methods in Anthropology*, London: AltaMira.

Salo, E., 2010. Men, women, temporality and critical ethnography in Africa – the imperative for a transdisciplinary conversation. *Anthropology Southern Africa*, *33*(3-4), pp.93-102.

Sanjek, R., 1990. A vocabulary for fieldnotes. *Fieldnotes: The makings of anthropology*, pp.92-121.

Sanjek, R., 1990. The secret life of fieldnotes. *Fieldnotes: The makings of anthropology*, pp.187-270.

Scarry, E., 1985. The body in pain: The making and unmaking of the world: Oxford University Press. *New York*.

Tsing, A.L., 2005. *Friction: An ethnography of global connection*. Princeton University Press.

Turner, V.W., 1973. Symbols in African ritual. Science, 179(4078), pp.1100-1105.

Turner, V., 1969. The ritual process: Structure and anti. Structure, 1966.

Veissière, S.P.L., 2018. "Toxic Masculinity" in the age of# MeToo: ritual, morality and gender archetypes across cultures. *Society and Business Review*, *13*(3), pp.274-286.

Waling A (2019a) Problematising "toxic" and "healthy" masculinity for addressing gender inequalities. Australian Feminist Studies 34(101): 362–375.

Wheaton, B. ed., 2004. *Understanding lifestyle sport: Consumption, identity and difference*. Routledge.

Online Sources

https://www.news24.com/news24/politics/on-the-road-green-fingered-upington-residents-are-

transforming-their-community-for-a-better-life-20240320
https://nonstopagainstapartheid.wordpress.com/2012/06/01/marching-to-save-the-lives-of-the-upington-14/
https://www.ofm.co.za/article/centralsa/331505/alcohol-abuse-young-people-in-northern-cape-particularly-vulnerable
https://www.statista.com/statistics/1129481/unemployment-rate-by-population-group-in-south-africa/
statsa.gov.za
https://www.safa.net/2023/12/28/broos-names-his-final-bafana-squad-for-the-africa-cup-of-nations-in-cote-divoire/
https://www.undp.org/south-africa/blog/harnessing-employability-south-africas-youth

www.ingramcontent.com/pod-product-compliance
Ingram Content Group UK Ltd.
Pitfield, Milton Keynes, MK11 3LW, UK
UKHW041956190726
13854UKWH00005B/2009

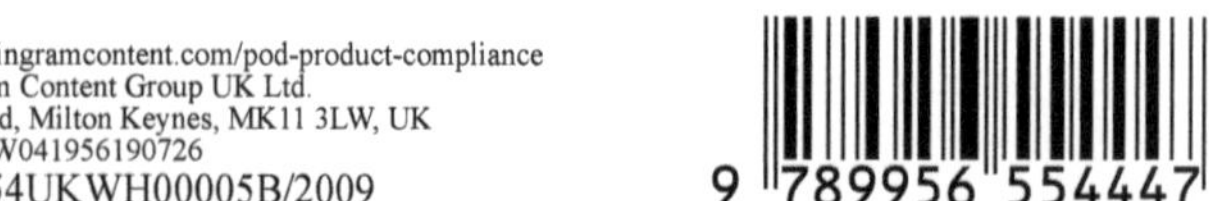

9 789956 554447